# A YEAR IN A DAY

KEN WELCH

# A YEAR IN A DAY
*My days in Vietnam 1968 – 1969*

PALMETTO
**PUBLISHING**
Charleston, SC
www.PalmettoPublishing.com

Copyright © 2024 by Ken Welch

All rights reserved

No portion of this book may be reproduced, stored in a retrieval system, or transmitted in any form by any means–electronic, mechanical, photocopy, recording, or other–except for brief quotations in printed reviews, without prior permission of the author.

Hardcover ISBN: 979-8-8229-4828-0
Paperback ISBN: 979-8-8229-4829-7

# Introduction

To all my readers:

My name is Kenneth R. Welch. I was born in Akron, Ohio in 1948. Moved to Evarts, Kentucky in Harlan County around 1952. I have eight brothers and sisters: Betty Jean, William Harold, Franklin Edward, Clarence Marvin, James Clayton, Mary Ellen, Beverly Sue and Sharon Annette. Son of Clarence and Mary Welch (Jump). In 1963, I moved to a city called Covington, Ky., where I met my wife Regina (Jeannie) Brownfield. We grew up together, went to the same High school, (Holmes High). I graduated in 1966, had numerous jobs, but really nothing that would keep me there, until I became a fireman in 1980. Ok, let's back up, so somewhere in the late 60's, not long after graduating high school, I managed to have my drivers license revoked!!! No real job to speak of. So, my thinking as a young man is, what am I gonna do without a driver's license, no job, and if I found one, how would I get there? City bus ??? Can't drive! I felt the only logical thing for me to do was to join the military. I chose the Army and with no further ado, that's what I did. Me at the age of 19 thinking, I'm gonna go in, get a good education and get out and find a good job. But, as you begin to read, that's not all, I got. Went through basic training in Fort Benning, Georgia. I'm feeling pretty good about my choice. Then, low and behold came to find out I was being shipped to Vietnam! No clue, as to what holds for me in that next year!! I'd be lying, if I said I wasn't a little nervous and apprehensive. But more of the unknown from day to day. Even though I wasn't in the Infantry front line, it didn't mean there was no danger of being attacked at any time day or night. There were land mines, snipers, rockets and Mortar attacks and many ways for them to get to you. Believe me, I consider myself a lucky one! I thank God every day for bringing me home to my family and the ones I loved and missed. You do have a family there, but it's a different family, my family there, we became Brothers! There, you were as thick as thieves. Had each other's back no matter the outcome. So, they are your family for that next year. And a family they were. I decided to keep a diary, so I would not forget those, who I became very close to and my experiences, good or bad. I would often say while writing in my diary, I'm gonna write a book someday of my experiences. Well, this is to honor all my buddies and to thank my friends and family for the support I have received over the years. I would like to say, in closing, it's a memory that is like burned into your brain, you don't realize the impact a war has on a person. Some good, some bad. Mine, just about the everyday life I spent over there. It has taken me a few years to finish what I had started, but they say it's never too late. I now reside in Mount Juliet, Tennessee, along with my wife Regina, my wonderful daughter Erin, her husband Luke and my wonderful son Nicholas. Along with our two awesome grandchildren Zalen and Jaylen. In advance, I would like to thank everyone for reading my biography, memoir in hopes you might understand each of the different roles our soldiers do, to keep us free. Thank You, Enjoy

## Day 2 May 13, 1968

I arrived in Long Binh about 8 pm last night. Had the details of filling sandbags most of today. After supper I was put on K.P. (kitchen police). Had to wash pots & pans. The minute I stepped off the plane last night the heat and humidity smacked me right in the face. This place has a strange smell to it. I've never smelt death before, but that's what I compare it to.

**Day 3 May 14, 1968**

I was put on detail again today. This time I had to go to the bunker line and re-build a bunker with sandbags. While we were there working, one of the guys got stung by a scorpion, he'll be OK. I found out today they are sending me to a place called Pleiku. It's in the central highlands of south Vietnam. I'll be with the 4th Infantry Division.

**Day 4 May 15, 1968**

Sent to Pleiku today, flew up here on a C-130 troop carrier. Camp Enari is the name of the 4th Infantry Division headquarters. I was processed in all day. Filling out paper work and other bull shit. They told us about all the different diseases we could catch while we are over here. I'll try to be careful. Ran upon one of my buddies from Ft. Gordon tonight. His name is Lennie Luncan, from Cincinnati Ohio. Right across the Ohio river from where I live, Covington, Kentucky, made PFC today.

**Day 5 May 16, 1968**

Today I had to pull K.P. at the Generals mess. This is the mess hall where all the officers from headquarters eat all these meals. Got a sunburn on my neck and arms. One good thing about their K.P. is I had very good food today. Didn't work too hard. I was the outside man, helped clean and washed the trash cans out. K.P. lasted from 6:00 AM until 10:00 pm. I am tired.

**Day 6 May 17, 1968**

Today was a repeat of yesterday, K.P. at General's mess, was outside again, got sunburn, and had good food again. Tired again.

**Day 7 May 18, 1968**

Had to go through some training with the M-16 rifle today. I found out today that I'll be with company A, of the 124th signal Battalion here in the 4th division. I can't wait to get there, so I can settle down.

**Day 8 May 19, 1968**

Went to church this morning. Had a class on the M-16. Had to learn how to disassemble and reassemble the M-16, and the important parts to keep clean at all times.

**Day 9 May 20, 1968**

I zeroed my weapon today, which means I got the sights set and fired it. I got paid $176.00 today. Went through the gas chamber today to make sure my mask worked correctly. Had a band at the NCO club tonight. The songs they sang reminded me of my little doll Jeannie.

**Day 10 May 21, 1968**

I finished training today. Moved to my regular unit this evening. Company A, 124th signal Battalion 4th Infantry division. So far, all the guys here seem to be alright. One of my buddies from Fort Gordon is here with me. His name is Wilbert McDowell, a soul brother.

**Day 11 May 22, 1968**

My first real day in my regular unit. I am in the cable section of the company. Helped load some reels of cable onto a truck. Straightened up some of my records, and got some of my equipment from S-4 today.

**Day 12 May 23, 1968**

Helped build a bunker in the motor pool. Had to pull guard duty in the motor pool bunker tonight with Wilbert. Me and Wilbert slept during guard duty. The bunkers are only a secondary line of bunkers. On guard from 1:30–7.00.

**Day 13 May 24, 1968**

Stood around in the motor pool all day doing nothing. Had guard duty again tonight 8:00–1:30. Slept again on guard.

**Day 14 May 25, 1968**

Had to march in a parade today. Had to dig some holes for telephone poles. Had A&R this afternoon. We got a new battalion commander today. The old one was a son-of-a-bitch. The new one seems to be alright.

The holes I had to dig were behind our company area. The Red Cross girls were in the mess hall today. We played baseball. It was fun.

**Day 15 May 26, 1968**

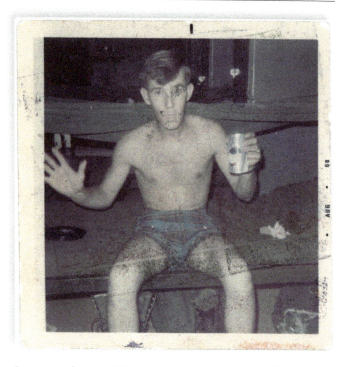

I was on the trouble team today with Sgt. Hill and PFC Coldwell. Had to replace a line from a terminal to the motor pool. Had guard duty in the motor pool from 8:00–2:00. Took some pictures today in the billets.

**Day 16 May 27, 1968**

Had to burn shit today. I was the shit burner today. All the shit comes from the company latrine and the cans from the South Vietnamese latrine. Boy you should have seen their shit, it was running over the edges of the can and filled with maggots. The smell almost made me sick.

**Day 17 May 28, 1968**

Went upon Dragon Mountain to help build a bunker for guard duty today. Had half the day off to get ready for my first real guard duty tonight on the bunker line. It's in bunker 115. Didn't do too much work on the mountain, just laid around and read a book.

**Day 18 May 29, 1968**

Had the day off today, because of guard duty last night. It got pretty cold last night, because it rained most of the night. Charlie didn't show up, which is a good thing Wilbert and Johnson were with me. I had the first shift from 6:00–8:00, and then 12:00–2:00. Bunker 115.

**Day 19 May 30, 1968**

I was supposed to go on a convoy. But they didn't need me. Helped put up an antenna today. Helped build a sidewalk in the company area. Had to climb a pole for the first time over here, and boy I was nervous as hell, but I did alright.

**Day 20 May 31, 1968**

Had to go to Dak To today. Flew up on a C-130 airplane the ride up here was great. There is some beautiful country over here. I had to wait until 12:30 to get a flight. This place, Dak To is known to have been one of the biggest battles over her in Vietnam. I am with some of the guys from my company A. The battle of Dak To November, 67.

**Day 21 June, 1, 1968**
Had to go up on hill 881. They want me to learn how to operate a radio. The 101st Airborne is up here. In the last two days I went from a billets, to a tent, to a bunker. I don't know anything about operating a radio, but I guess I'll learn. Boy, you should see this place. It looks like a big forest fire has been here. The 101st took over this hill back in November '67.

**Day 22 June 2, 1968**
Sent a message to Terror 10 and received one from Terror 13. I had to operate the radio from 12:00 to 8:00. There isn't much to operate a radio. It rained today and flooded our bunker and our generators. Had to dig a trench around our bunker.

**Day 23 June 3, 1968**
I slept all day, because I had the radio last night. Didn't do much on the radio, there weren't any messages all night. Today was Wilberts birthday.

**Day 24 June 4, 1968**

Had to go back down to Dak To today. Had to take one of the generators to get fixed. Played some poker with some of the guys and won $7.00. Slept most of the day.

**Day 25 June 5, 1968**

Still in Dak To. I got my first letter from home today, three from Jeannie and one from mom. Boy, was I glad to get them. Didn't do much today except read and sleep.

**Day 26 June 6, 1968**

Still in Dak To. Doing nothing but sitting around doing nothing. I haven't done any work since I've been out here.

**Day 27 June 7, 1968**

Went back up to hill 881 with the generator. Picked up my clothes and went back down. Had to help put up a tent today. Played cards and won $39.00 from Pfc. Holmes, a soul brother.

**Day 28 June 8, 1968**

Had an alert today. I sent Jeannie $25.00 to put in the bank. Lost $30.00 in a poker game, to Sgt. Carter. Had Jeannie too start a savings account for us.

**Day 29 June 9, 1968**

Didn't do anything today. They brought the jeep up to the tent that got hit on a convey yesterday. One guy was killed and two other guys were shot. Lost $20.00 to Sgt. Carter.

**Day 30 June 10, 1968**

Went downtown Dak To today. Was put on a sandbag detail. One of the guys bought a monkey while we were in Dak To. Its name is JoJo. Today was the first day I did any work since I've been here in Dak To.

**Day 31 June 11, 1968**

Didn't do anything except read and sleep today. Had to stand watch to make sure some of the guys didn't take any of our phones with them. They were in trailers.

**Day 32 June 12, 1968**

Had to pull motor stables on a ¾-ton truck today. Had to pick up all the phones in the company area. Had to take all of the phone lines from the poles and climbed my first telephone pole. We're supposed to go back to base camp tomorrow. Boy, I hope we never go back.

**Day 33 June 13, 1968**

Left Dak To today, back to base camp by convoy. Didn't see any charlies on the way. I had a great time going back. Some of the guys tried to get me to smoke some of their grass, but I told them I didn't want any.

**Day 34 June 14, 1968**

I was off today. Straightened up my locker. Well, I'm back where the shit flies. They've made a couple of changes since I've been gone. Like shining my boots every day and shaving every day. Which I think is a bunch of bull shit.

**Day 35 June 15, 1968**

Had to work on Dragon Mountain. Had A&R today. Got my glasses and mail from the field today. I got two regular pair and one pair of sunglasses. The Red Cross girls were over to the mess hall, but I didn't go over.

**Day 36 June 16, 1968**

Went to church this morning. Had to help put sandbags around a building. Worked in the motor pool painting numbers on the bumpers of our trucks and jeeps.

**Day 37 June 17, 1968**

Worked in the motor pool. Had the afternoon off because of guard duty on Dragon mountain. It was quiet all night. Boy it sure got cold last night. The fog rolled in early last night, and boy you couldn't see ten feet in front of you.

**Day 38 June 18, 1968**

I had the first half of the day off. Worked in the motor pool painting tools.

**Day 39 June 19, 1968**

Was on the trouble team today. Had a USO show at the NCO club. Peggy William, a dancer on ShinDig. Boy, it was really nice. Had to put a new line on my company phone today.

**Day 40 June 20, 1968**

Had to pull motor stable on A-96. Worked on bunker on Dragon mountain. Helped fill sandbags.

**Day 41 June 21, 1968**

Had to dig up grass and replant it in the company area. Got four blisters on my left hand. Boy this shit they're making us do is making me sick. This is the sorriest damn place over here in Vietnam.

**Day 42 June 22, 1968**

Had an alert this morning at 6:00 until 7:00. Then, I had K.P. the rest of the day. The South Vietnamese did most of the work. I only had to wash the supper dishes.

**Day 43 June 23, 1968**

Went to Qui Nhon, there I went swimming in the South China Sea at Red Beach. Went downtown and Boy, I had the best time since I've been over here. I went to the bar in Quin Nhon, and had a couple drinks with my buddies.

Kennie & Wilbert

**Day 44 June 24, 1968**

Had to load cargo onto trucks. Then, I went to Red Beach for about three hours. Took some pictures. Then we rode around downtown. Didn't have a chance to get any leg, because I didn't have any money.

**Day 45 June 25, 1968**

Got back to base camp today. Got some letters from Jeannie telling me she got a job at Frisch's in Ft. Mitchell. I don't like the idea of her working there but, it is a job and she can help save money for our future. Today, was the first day I wrote in this diary, because I got it today from Miss Jeannie Brownfield.

**Day 46 June 26, 1968**

Had the first half of the day off and went to the rifle range to zero my rifle (M-16). Fired the M-60 machine gun, and the M-79 grenade launcher. Had to plant some more grass. This planting of grass every day is making me sick.

**Day 47 June 27, 1968**

Had to dig holes and plant some more grass today. Got 6 blisters on my hands and also had to load some sandbags. Some of the guys tried to get me to smoke some grass. They started giving out passes today. About twenty guys got them to go to Pleiku.

**Day 48 June 28, 1968**

We got a new company commander today. Had to go up on Dragon Mountain today to help build a walkway for the bunker. I didn't do too much work because my left hand was hurting. The blisters I got yesterday busted and boy do they hurt. Then this afternoon I had to put some more dirt in the walkway to the NCO club.

**Day 49 June 29, 1968**

Well, today was a pretty good day. I only made one formation and that was the 6:00 AM formation. I was the billets guard this morning. After lunch I had to go over to the com-center to tear down a wall. Then we had A&R. The C.O. gave us the rest of the day off. This is the first day in a long time that we didn't have a 6:00 PM work call. I pulled 30 minutes C.Q. runner for Sgt. Buchanan while he took a shower.

**Day 50 June 30, 1968**

Went to church this morning. After church, I got paid $180.00. They only paid me E-2 pay, when I was supposed to get E-3 pay. Had to go up on Dragon Mountain to finish the walkway to the bunker. The good thing about it was we didn't have any NCO's with us to tell us what to do. I had a 6:00 o'clock work call, and had to plant some more grass in the company area.

**Day 51 July 1, 1968**

Went on sick call today for my back. The doctor only gave me some pills to take, one every four hours. When I got back I had to go up to S-4 for Sgt. Duncan to trade some mosquito nets. This afternoon I had to build handrails to the bunker upon Dragon Mountain. Then at the 6:00 o'clock work call, I had to tag the gas mask in the supply room.

**Day 52 July 2, 1968**

Had to mark our boots, belts, and helmets today. Worked over at the com-center. Had to remove a Conex. Had to build a wall around the Conex also. Went to the post office to get three money orders, and send Jeannie's package home. Lost a dollar to Sgt. Braggs playing nine ball pool.

**Day 53 July 3, 1968**

Well, today was a very easy one, I had billets orderly today. All I had to do was sweep the floor, and straighten up lockers and bunk beds. Got my first letter from my sister Betty today. Have C.Q. runner tonight, get tomorrow off.

### Day 54 July 4, 1967

Well today was a fairly good 4th because I was off today, because I was the C.Q. runner last night. All I had to do was operate the switchboard, wake up the K.P.'s and cooks. I had C.Q. runner for Sgt Jones. Went to bed about 7:30 and got up at 12:00. Then I went over to the P.X. After that, I just laid around all day and read a joke book. I got the book I've been looking for today. In cold blood (by Truman Capote) saw the movie at Ft. Gordon, Ga.

### Day 55 July 5, 1968

Had to go up on Dragon Mountain to help build a bunker. Had the last half of the day off. Because I have guard duty tonight on the mountain. I pulled guard duty on the bunker line with Wilbert and Jones. Had to trade with Conklin because he looked too dirty. Sgt. Beavers was Sgt. of the guard, he's also my platoon Sgt. and had Sgt. Jones on the guard.

## Day 56 July 6, 1968

Didn't get much sleep last night because Wilbert kept me up, bull-shitting all night. Had guard duty from 7–9 and 1–3. Had to stay at the bunker and was on police call this morning. This afternoon we had a battalion party. Boy, I had a great time. Our company played a game of softball, and tug of war with three other companies, and of course we won them all. Sgt. Duncan even had me jumping rope. Sgt. Smith our acting 1st Sgt only an E-7 made 1st Sgt (E-8) at the ceremonies. Really had a great time. Lost about $40.00 in a poker game (black jack) tonight.

### Day 57 July 7, 1968
Today I worked for 1st Sgt Smith building fire boxes for the billets. Johnson and I made 15 of them, have to make 7 more tomorrow, and then paint them. Got a good tan today. Today was the longest I've worked since I've been here, from 7:00 in the morning until 4:30, and then from 5:00 until 7:00.

### Day 58 July 8, 1968
Found out today, I get to go before the board to become a Specialist Fourth class on the 10th. Got a new job today, as a company carpenter. Bought a polaroid camera today for $100.00. Sister Sharon wrote to me today, telling me mom broke her leg. Worked for Sgt Duncan painting the fire boxes I built yesterday.

### Day 59 July 9, 1968
Had to nail up all the fireboxes on the billets today. Then I shined my boots for when I go up before the board tomorrow. I took some pictures with my camera today. A couple of them messed up, but the rest of them came out pretty good. Boy I should consider

myself lucky for getting this new job. I don't have to pull guard duty, K.P., patrols or convoys. Shaved my mustache off today for the board.

### Day 60 July 10, 1968

Built a box for our mail man today. Didn't do much more work. Went before the board for Specialist 4 today. Hope I did well. Have to work in the orderly room tonight. Remodel it.

### Day 61 July 11, 1968

I was off all day today. Had to work in the supply room last night, didn't do much work, went over to the mess hall and drank some coffee and bullshitted with some of the night cooks. Slept until 2:00 today. Drank some EarlyTime whiskey straight in Sgt. James room, with Wilbert, James, and Sparks all soul brothers. Worked in the motor pool during workcall.

## Day 62 July 12, 1968

Was off again today, because I worked in the supply room last night. Wilbert bought a tape recorder today. I took some pictures with my camera. I have to work in the supply room again tonight. We have a foot and wall locker inspection tomorrow. Working on the billets right now. Saw the movie Grand Prix tonight, it's a very good movie.

## Day 63 July 13, 1968

Was off today, because I worked again last night. Worked until about 3:20 AM. Nailed up some wire. Didn't do much today except lay around and read in cold blood and took some more pictures. We didn't have the inspection today. We also didn't have a work call. We will sleep in tomorrow.

## Day 64 July 14, 1968

Got to sleep late this morning. Went to church. Had a lecture from Sgt. Major of our Battalion on why we are beautifying the area. Worked in the day room putting up a new ceiling with Johnson. Didn't have any work-call again today. Today was moms birthday.

**Day 65 July 15, 1968**

Worked in the day room this morning and at the 6:00 o'clock work call. This afternoon, I worked in the orderly room, remodeling. Found out today, they took me off the board, because they didn't have orders on me being a PFC. I came out third on the board out of eighteen. They are supposed to type up my orders at the division headquarters, and change my date. Then I'll be put back on the board again. Won $12.50 playing blackjack tonight.

## Day 66 July 16, 1968

I had to nail some of the roofs back on the billets, then cleaned up the day room. Put up a phone on the outside of the orderly room. This afternoon I was in charge of the Montagnard pronounced as (mountain yard) kids cutting grass. Bought a watch off one of them for $10.00. We had an alert last night at about 9:30. Won $6.00 last night playing cards. Broke 300 days today, down to 299 days left. Today was the sixth day I haven't heard from Jeannie.

## Day 67 July 17, 1968

Davis + Kramer on LRB Mt.

Base Camp

Today Sgt. Duncan didn't have anything for me to do this morning. So I went up on Dragon Mountain to help build a bunker and took some pictures. This afternoon I had to fix the seats in the latrine, then I put a new screen and plastic cover over our shower rooms. During work call, I put a top on our day room. Had a show at the NCO club tonight, wasn't bad.

### Day 68 July 18, 1968
Got me a new helper today, Wilbert McDowell. We had to cut some lumber for the orderly room today. Had to put a fire box in front of the day room. Have to work in the orderly room tonight.

### Day 69 July 19, 1968
Well I was off the first half of the day, because I worked last night. I only worked about 30 minutes but I told Sgt. Duncan we worked about 4 hours, so I could get this morning off and I did. I only cut some 1 × 4 boards today. Layed around the billets. Right now the whole company is getting ready to go on a patrol. About 80% of the division is going. Everybody in my company is going. I am in the Sgt. Lawrence squad. If anything happens to me on this patrol, let Jeannie Brownfield know I died loving her very much.

## Day 70 July 20, 1968

Well, I had to get up at 3:30 am, because the whole company went on patrol. Boy, am I tired. It seemed like we walked about 35 miles all together, with our packs and M-16. One guy from C-company got lost. They're sending out a patrol tomorrow to try and find him. Didn't see any sign of Charlie. I enjoyed the workout, but it was a walk and a half. I am very tired right now.

**Day 71 July 21, 1968**

Wilbert and I had to start building our little park in the company area, we marked it off and cut some of the stakes. Didn't have workcall today. Went to church this morning. Wilbert and I taped some records tonight. We acted like dis-jockeys from L. A. and Cincinnati stations KGFJ & WSAI.

**Day 72 July 22, 1968**

Worked on our project today. Got most of it laid out. Built a shelf for a new E-6 during work call. Got four letters today. One from Jeannie, Sue, Sharon and one from mom.

**Day 73, July 23, 1968**

Today Wilbert and I had to dig a hole for the new pisser. Then I had to work by myself for the rest of the day, because Wilbert has guard duty tonight. I had to dig the old pisser up. During, work call I had to build some hand rails for a bridge. We don't have any lights tonight, so I am going to bed early. I had to take an ice cold shower tonight, ok, but as long as I get clean.

### Day 74 July 24, 1968

Didn't do much this morning because I had to go fire my M-16 at the rifle range. I also fired the M-60, and M-79. Had to put the canvas back on the roof of the day room where the wind blew it off. Wilbert and I finished the staking of our patio during workcall.

### Day 75 July 25, 1968

Boy it rained all day today. I had to dig a trench in front of the latrine so the water could run into the ditch. I had to change my boots and clothes. I was so wet! Then I had to work on the mess hall, build on extra room. Put some tar on the roof. Then I had to put two windows in the day room. During work call I had to put the canvas back on the day room roof, and put some plastic over the door. Yes, the monsoon season is here.

### Day 76 July 26, 1968

Well, today I got fucked out of SP/4, but the son-of-a-bitches finally gave me my orders for Pfc. I am getting so goddamn sick of getting screwed, it's going to cause my death one of these days. I didn't do much work today except patch up a window, clean a ditch, and put up a drain in the mess hall. I am getting sick of this goddamn army life. I feel as though I am going to crack up one of these days.

### Day 77 July 27, 1968
Today wasn't too bad because it didn't rain all day. I had to watch the Montagnard kids while they dug out a ditch. I had to patch up some windows and holes in the day room. I am still pissed off about yesterday. I have to work in the mess hall tonight, painting it.

### Day 78 July 28, 1968
I was off today because I worked in the mess hall. Last Night, Wilbert and I had to paint. I got up around 12:00 today. We moved our bunks around today. We made double bunks. Sgt. Duncan told Wilbert and me one of us is going to have to move to battalion headquarters to live. But I think he's going to get someone else. I am working in the mess hall right now. I smoked some pot tonight for the first time in my life. Tony has some more, so me and him are going to smoke it later. Right now, I am getting ready to write to my love Jeannie. Finished in cold blood today. Didn't get high off the pot.

## Day 79 July 29, 1968

Today is my dad's birthday. Happy birthday dad. I had to paint in the mess hall last night. I was supposed to have the day off, but I only had half the day off. I had to help build that room onto the mess hall. I have to take K.P. for Robinson tomorrow, because Sgt. Duncan is sending him to the battalion and boy am I glad. They had a show at the club tonight, I had a few beers.

## Day 80 July 30, 1968

I had K.P. today and boy I worked my ass off. Today I received my sheets from the laundry and tonight will be the first night I'll get to sleep in a bed with clean sheets since I've been here in Vietnam. Tomorrow is payday.

## Day 81 July 31, 1968

Today was payday and I drew $200.00. Had to give up $100.00 for my camera I bought. Wilbert and I had to tear down our old woodshack and build another one. Have to paint in the mess hall tonight. The Red Cross girls gave me a birthday card today.

**Day 82 August 1, 1968**

I was off most of the day, because I worked in the mess hall last night. Went over to the PX and post office. Put some tar on the roof of the day room this afternoon. Lost $10.00 in a poker game tonight. Got my first letter from my brother Bill today. Today was Jeannie's moms birthday.

**Day 83 August 2, 1968**

Me and Wilbert had to paint the day room today. Have to go on a two-day patrol tomorrow. Won $10.00 in a card game tonight. If anything happens to me on the patrol, let Jeannie know I love her very much.

**Day 84 August 3, 1968.**

Well, I had to go on a patrol today. We stopped at a village, then proceeded on with the patrol. We walked about a mile into the jungle, and then came back. I was the right flank man. Then, we had to go to the Medcap Village to stay all night. We didn't see any Charlies. Boy, it rained hard all night and I had to sleep in a puddle of water. I had to pull guard duty with Wilbert and Sgt. Jones, both are soul brothers. We bullshitted until about 12:00 and then started pulling guard, I had the last shift 4 to 6.

## Day 85 August 4, 1968

Well, today we had to make one long sweep around the village. I had to carry the radio and boy it was heavy after a while. After we got back, me, Wilbert, Inhoff and our medic Kennedy went down to the first village we came to. Ate me some roasted corn a mama-son made for me. Then we had to go on another patrol around the village. We fixed our tent over our bunker so we wouldn't get wet and we didn't.

**Day 86 August 5, 1968**

Well we got back today. Had the day off. Cleaned my weapon, took a shower, and then went to bed. Lost

$10.00 earlier today, and another $8.00 tonight playing cards.

### Day 87 August 6, 1968
Well today was pretty easy. The first half of the day I had to be the barracks orderly, all I did was sweep the billets. I had the second half off because I have guard duty tonight. They were supposed to have two men make the man, but they only picked one, otherwise I would have gotten the man.

### Day 88 August 7, 1968

Well guard was pretty good last night. It didn't rain much, but it got pretty cool. I had to pull two shifts, first one from 11p to 1a, then from 5a to 7a. I had the first half of the day off, so I slept all morning. Helped Sgt. Jones take some lumber to the burn pit. Had to unload a truck load of gravel during workcall. Have K.P. tomorrow.

**Day 89 August 8, 1968**

Had K.P. today, I didn't work too much until the supper dishes, then I really had to hump. Got off about 7:30, I hate K.P.

**Day 90 August 9, 1968**

Had to put some new sandbags on bunker 113. Then, I had to plant some pine trees in the company area. Then, I had to put some more tar on the day room, again! Sgt. Beavers was supposed to have me work late tonight, but he didn't. Lost $9.00 in a card game tonight.

**Day 91 August 10, 1968**

Well, today I had to finish painting the day room. Then I had to get ready to pull guard duty in bunker 115. The barrel of my weapon was dirty and because of that I didn't make the man.

**Day 92 August 11, 1968**

Well, guard duty was hard last night, because we had a ⅔ rd alert (expecting Charlie). I had the first watch from 7p to 9p, then had to pull guard duty from 1a to 3:30a, because of the alert. It got a little cool last night. I was off this morning and all I did was sleep. Then I got up and cleaned my weapon. Was off all day until about 6:00 then I had to go to A-74 (total inspection) but that only took me about thirty minutes.

**Day 93 August 12, 1968**

Well Sgt. Duncan had me guard a truck in the motor pool last night. It had 60 cases of cigarettes on it. I had to guard it from 8 to 1. I stole four cartons of viceroy, ten towels, and four new T-shirts. I had to guard it again this morning from 7 to 9. Was off most of the day, but had to haul some gravel during workcall.

**Day 94 August 13, 1968**

Today, I had to go on a convoy to pick up some gravel. Didn't do much during workcall. Had to go down and replace a phone in bunkers 111 and 116. Had a show at the club tonight. All girls, they were really good, there were eight of them.

# Day 95 August 14, 1968

Today me and Dalton had to go on a gravel run, but we didn't get past the M.P. stop. We had to wait until a convoy was to come by, but it never came by so we had to return to the company. I bought two Montagnard shirts from the kids on the side of the road. Had the afternoon off because of guard duty on the mountain.

**Day 96 August 15, 1968**

Boy, guard was a bitch last night. I got soaked with rain and so did my sleeping bag. I was wet and cold all night long. We didn't get off the mountain until about 1:00 this afternoon, because of the fog. I was off the rest of the day. Have to be C.Q. runner tonight for Sgt. Carter. Have tomorrow off.

**Day 97 August 16, 1968**

I was off today, because of me being the C.Q. runner last night. Played cards with Pfc. Grantham and Sgt. Carter. Had to operate the switchboard and I had to go get two guys for guard duty, because the division was on a ⅔rd alert tonight. Typed Jeannie a letter and addressed some envelopes with the typewriter. During workcall today I had to put a baseboard around the day room.

**Day 98 August 17, 1968**

Today I had to go on another gravel run. Had to help unload the gravel after lunch. Then I had to put up some walls made of wood in the day room. I bought myself a tape recorder from Dalton last night for $80.00. I sent Jeannie a tape from it tonight.

**Day 99 August 18, 1968**

Well today, I had to go zero (fire) my weapon. Then I cleaned my weapon. This afternoon I told Sgt. Beavers I had to clean my weapon, so he gave me the rest of the day off. Went over to company C and watched a movie, The good, The bad and The ugly.

## Day 100 August 19, 1968

Today is my 100th day over here in this God forsaken place. I have 265 days to go, which seems like a long time. I had to go out last night to replace a line on the bunker line. I got to bed about 1:30. I slept until 6:30 this morning. Me, Robinson and Sgt. Carter had to run a new line this morning. This afternoon I had to work for Sgt. Duncan. Made a petition in the day room. During the workcall I had to pick beer cans out of a trash can behind the EM club and then smash them and put them in a hole and cover with dirt.

## Day 101 August 20, 1968

Well they came and got me last night for guard duty because there was a ⅔'s alert. They were expecting Charlie last night, but he didn't show up. There's supposed to be a Battalion of them out there. We had tanks and all kinds of good shit waiting for him. I had to pull three shifts last night. Only got four hours of sleep. Had to build another petition for the day room. We have to stay in the infiltration bunker tonight. Got a letter from one of my buddies from basic training today. Otis Thomas, with the 82nd airborne division.

## Day 102 August 21, 1968

I was lucky last night, I only had to pull one shift 6p to 9p. The battalion commander came around checking. Had to go on a gravel run with Dalton, but we didn't have to go because they said we don't need any more gravel. Then I was put on the trouble team, but we didn't have any trouble so we did nothing. After lunch I had to go down and fix a wall on one of the bunkers (112) that fell down last night. Right now I am on C.Q. again with Sgt. Barria. I am supposed to get off tomorrow. But the way they are around here I don't know if I will or not.

## Day 103 August 22, 1968

C.Q. wasn't too bad last night, I fell asleep a couple of times. We didn't get the company up until 6:00 o'clock this morning because the Sgt. and I were asleep. We've had black outs for the last three nights now, because of Charlie being close by. I am supposed to go before the board tomorrow. I had all day off today. I shined my boots, ironed my fatigues. I shaved my mustache off tonight. I have a 2nd shift on the infiltration bunker tonight.

**Day 104 August 23, 1968**

Today is my birthday. I am 20 years old. On My birthday, I had to man the bunker in the motor pool last night from 4 to 7:30, but I only went to sleep. I went before the board again today for Sp/4. I don't think I did too good because of Sgt. Beavers asked me some questions I've never heard of, then I went to sleep. Charlie was outside the wire today so we had an alert. They killed 11 of them last night on the other side of base camp. They hit all the places close to us last night. They're supposed to hit us real hard within the next few days. Have to man the bunker again tonight, 6–9, 12–3.

**Day 105 August 24, 1968**

Well I was supposed to have K.P. today, but I had to build some more petitions for the day room. Well while I was working, I cut a small portion of my left thumb off. Boy did it hurt. I went down to the 4th medical hospital to get it bandaged up. It looks like something had chewed it up. While I was down there they brought in a Charlie who had been shot in the leg. All I did this evening was wipe off the tables, while on K.P. Got a birthday card from my brother Marv. Have to go back to the 4th med tomorrow.

## Day 106 August 25, 1968

Well we got to sleep in this morning. I didn't do anything the rest of the morning. After lunch I had to go and get a new bandage on my hand. My thumb has been bleeding all night and day. When I got back I was supposed to help Sgt. Duncan, build another petition in the day room. But I didn't do any work, I just sat around and watched him work. I didn't do anything else the rest of the day. It's been a week since I've heard from Miss Brownfield but I don't give a damn if I never hear from her again. I am going to reconsider marrying her when I get home.

## Day 107 August 26, 1968

Today I was on the trouble team, I didn't do any work though. This afternoon I had to go to the 4th med to get a clean bandage. I have to go back again tomorrow. They gave me a tetanus shot today. When I got back I helped Sgt. Duncan in the day room. Then Sgt. Beavers and I had to go down and put some trip flares in front of bunker 113. I helped Sgt. Duncan again during work call. I got birthday cards from mom, Jeannie, Kewp, Sharon, Marty, Rhonda, and Debbie today.

## Day 108 August 27, 1968

Sgt. Duncan and myself worked in the day room and his room all day. He keeps telling me my shit is good. I had to get a new bandage on my thumb. Got a card from my sister Betty today. Sgt. Duncan gave me a numbered paint set today, it's really nice. I have to go back to 4th med tomorrow.

### Day 109 August 28, 1968

Well, me and Sgt. Ducan made a frame for the ping pong table. That's all we did in the day room except put a couple of tables together. I had to go back down to 4th med to get my bandage changed. Didn't do anything during workcall.

### Day 110 August 29, 1968

Well today I had to help put up a sign. I also had to rebuild four bridges in the company area this morning. Had to go back down to 4th med this afternoon. The guy put a bad bandage on my thumb. I didn't do anything this afternoon but paint my picture. Had to put my tools away during workcall and throw away some boards. I saw the movie Good, Bad and Ugly tonight over at Company C. Got a package from Mr. Brownfield today. Had some pillow cases, candy and some spray, and also got a birthday card.

## Day 111 August 30, 1968
Well I got paid today $213.00. I owed most of it out, and lost the rest of it playing cards. I didn't do anything the rest of the morning. Went to 4th med and had guard duty on the bunker line tonight.

## Day 112 August 31, 1968
Well I traded the line for the mountain last night. It didn't rain at all last night and the fog wasn't too bad either. Got off the mountain about 8:30 and then cleaned my weapon. Went to the 4th med again today. Helped Sgt. Duncan in the old PX building. Had to build a petition. Helped him during work call also. Got my card from Jeannie today with all my friends' signatures on it. Boy, I smoked about three cigarettes full of grass last night and I felt so good. I also imagined in my mind things like oceans, deserts, and cities. So if you want to feel good, get some grass.

**Day 113 September 1, 1968**

Well we got to sleep until 8:00 this morning. Went to church. Went back down to 4th med. Went to the post office and the PX. Didn't do anything the rest of the day.

**Day 114 September 2, 1968**

Got high on the grass again last night. Boy that stuff sure does you a job. I had to work in the motor pool today. Went to 4th med. Helped paint in the motor pool. Tore up a truck.

**Day 115 September 3, 1968**

Boy I went on a trip last night that was out of this world. I had so much last night, I could still feel it today. I had to work in the motor pool all day, but I didn't do any work. Today was the last day I have to go to the 4th med. I had to put some concertina wire in front of the bunker and on the bunker line also today. The guys who went on a trip with me last night were Sgt. Bragg, John, Baxter, Dean Olson and Jones. We also sniffed some vicks nasal spray, which will also give you a good trip.

## Day 116 September 4, 1968

I had to pull motor stables on an A-59, 2½ ton truck and that was the first time in a long time, since I pulled motor stables. This afternoon, I had to help Sgt. Tribune clean the M-17's (gas masks). Had to rewire the old PX building with Jones (my grass buddy) and Sgt. Beavers during work call. I am supposed to get my military drivers license tomorrow.

## Day 117 September 5, 1968

This morning, I had to help load a 2½ ton truck. While Sgt. Barria was driving down to the bunker line and he ran off the road into a ditch throwing me into the steering wheel. It Didn't hurt. I was off this afternoon because I have guard duty on the mountain, but I exchanged with Conklin for the line. I made the man today for the first time, but they have a ⅔ alert, so I have to pull guard duty tonight.

## Day 118 September 6, 1968

Boy guard was a bitch last night. It was cold and windy as hell. I had to go back down to the bunker line this morning to check all of the wire in front of the bunker. After lunch I cleaned my weapon. Did nothing the rest of the day, until supper. I had to go help put some sandbags around a Conex. They had a show at the EM club tonight. It was really good. I got a little nice on beer tonight.

### Day 119 September 7, 1968

Today, I had to go pick up 1300 sand-bags outside of Pleiku. The Montagnard kids loaded them for us. When we got back, we had to finish sandbagging the Conex over at Favor. After we got it built, the back wall fell down. During workcall, we had to go back over and build it back up, then, we had to police call the area. We finished at about 8:00. I got a letter from my buddy Otis Thomas from basic.

### Day 120 September 8, 1968

This morning I had to clean out the infiltration bunkers for the general inspection tomorrow. This afternoon I had to help clean the billets for the I. G. Didn't do anything the rest of the day. I traded my big tape recorder to Sgt. Beavers for two small ones.

### Day 121 September 9, 1968

Today I had to work in the motor pool all day. Just cleaned up all the tools, trucks, and things like that. We have the inspection tomorrow instead of today.

During work call me and Sgt Jones had to fix a screen on the latrine.

**Day 122 September 10, 1968**
Well, today I didn't do much. I was billet's orderly, because of the I.G. (Inspection General) that never came around. They are supposed to come tomorrow. I am taping Wilbert records tonight.

**Day 123 September 11, 1968**
I was Billets orderly again this morning until after lunch. They never did inspect us, so the I. G. is over and I am glad. After lunch I was on the trouble team, and had to take down the extra wire on the bunker line. I didn't get off until about 10:30 tonight. Sgt. Buchanan ran into a hole in the road and threw me around like a rubber ball. I got a couple of bumps and bruises out of it, plus I lost my glasses and hat.

**Day 124 September 12, 1968**
Well Charlie hit us last night, but none of the rounds got inside base camp. They all hit outside. Wilbert and I had to man the bunker in the motor pool. We got to sleep until 7:30 this morning because of the alert, only this one was for real. I found my glasses this morning,

they weren't broken. Had to go up on the mountain to repair a cable but I just slept in the back of the truck while the other guys fixed it. Off this afternoon because I have guard on the mountain tonight.

### Day 125 September 13, 1968

Well I made the man yesterday but they had a ⅔ alert so I had to go down on the bunker line at 5:30. It rained a little on guard. This morning I had to help build a key box for the 1st Sgt. I got my records from Jeannie last night. I was off the rest of the afternoon and all I did was paint and record records.

### Day 126 September 14, 1968

Well I got blown away on grass last night, I still feel it today. I have K.P. tonight. Had to help put some spiraled cable back on some poles on Dragon mountain. While we were up there two choppers were bringing smoke on a Revene. This afternoon they didn't have anything for me to do which is very surprising. So I just sat around and bullshitted with some of the guys. The Donut Dollies were over at the mess hall today. I sold my records for $40.00. I am on K.P. right now off tomorrow. I'm supposed to get a little nice on pot tonight with Jones and the new cook.

**Day 127 September 15, 1968**

Well I was off today for having K.P. last night. I got blown away on pot last night. Boy that was the best trip I've taken yet. Went to the post office to mail Sgt. Sparks screen to him.

**Day 128 September 16, 1968**

Had to work in the motor pool this morning. Pulled motor stables on a couple of ¾ ton's. This afternoon I had to work on an ammo bunker down on the line next to bunker 114. Got a sunburn on my arms and back. Bought me a radio and record player in one today from Holmes for $15.00.

**Day 129 September 17, 1968**

We had an alert last night, and it was for real. It was a ground attack. Charlie killed two G.I.'s with a rocket. They were in bunker 53, on the other side of base camp. They hit about 3:00 AM last night. This morning we went to sleep until 7:00. I had to grease all the batteries in all of our trucks this morning. This afternoon I had to help load some wire in front of our bunkers. Had to help unload a truck after chow tonight. Got Jeannie's senior picture today and she's beautiful in it.

## Day 130 September 18, 1968

Well today I had to take my test for my drivers license, I passed with flying colors. Had to pull motor stables on a ¾ ton also. After lunch I had to go take my eye test. Went to the PX, but it was closed because of a power failure in the area. Have guard on the bunker line tonight. Made the man again today for the third time in a row. Didn't have to go on guard until 7:00. Have a show at the club tonight, but I'll have to miss it.

**Day 131 September 19, 1968**

Well it was quiet last night, and dry. Somebody hit us with tear gas about 12:00, but they didn't know who it was. They were fighting with Charlie on the other side of base camp, but he didn't bother us at all. Had all day off, went to the PX, and rode around with Jones. Just messed around and did nothing all day.

## Day 132 September 20, 1968

Worked in the motor pool all day today. Worked on a 3/4 ton truck, number 24 all day getting it ready for the inspection tomorrow. Got filthy cleaning the damn thing. Didn't get off until 9:00 tonight, because I was on trouble team. I'll probably have to go back out tonight, but I sure hope I don't.

**Day 133 September 21, 1968**

Just hung around in the motor pool cleaning things up for the inspection, we never did have it for some odd reason. I was off for the rest of the day.

**Day 134 September 22, 1968**

Well I got blasted last night. We got to sleep in this morning. Went to the rifle range this morning and cleaned my weapon this afternoon.

**Day 135 September 23, 1968**

Got blown away on pot last night, almost got caught so that means I have to cool it for a couple of days, Wilbert was with me. Today we had to move all the things from the Conex's to the old PX building, and boy I worked my ass off. I am working out a little every night.

## Day 136 September 24, 1968

I took my driver's test for my license today and passed. Get my license tomorrow. Had to help straighten up and clean up in the new line shack, that's about all I did today. Two of my buddies, Wilbert and Malloy, had to go see the old man today, because of some trouble they got into, he didn't do anything to them.

## Day 137 September 25, 1968

Got my licenses today. Had to help in the line shack. Had to T.I a couple of trucks, but they dead lined them. Was supposed to go downtown Pleiku but never did go. We have a sweep tomorrow. We have to sweep a village tomorrow. If anything happens to me, let Jeannie know I loved her.

## Day 138 September 26, 1968

Base Camp

Sweep

Today we went on another division sweep. We flew out by choppers. The walk was a very long one. We were suppose to search a village, but the stupid people in charge couldn't find it. We had to cross about three creeks, and one of them about three different times. The water was deep at some places. One time we had to climb a tree to get across. Didn't see any charlies. Found a couple of places where he had been before. Overall it was a pretty good sweep. I lost the watch Jeannie gave me for my 19th birthday.

## Day 139 September 27, 1968

Today was the first time I got to drive since I've been in the army. I drove one jeep. Had to take Sgt Trabue to S-4 and 16th artillery. Then Sgt Jones and myself had to take some gravel down to bunker 115. I was off this afternoon because I have guard on the mountain. I made the man today. Sgt Ball picked Dalton, but I challenged him and won. Had to go up to the battalion to stand inspection. I hope they don't call ⅔ alert.

## Day 140 September 28, 1968

Well they called a ⅔ alert last night about 6:30. Guard was alright, but I sure got sleepy during guard. I was off all day, and slept this morning until 12:00. They have a show at the NCO club tonight, and I am going to go.

## Day 141 September 29, 1968

Well I went to the show last night and got drunker than a skunk. The show was really good. I took a shower last night at about 12:00, which made four for the day. We got to sleep in this morning. Went to church this morning, then went to the Red Cross headquarter to get some records. Had to put some poles in the ground behind our line shack. Tomorrow is payday. I think I get my SP/4 orders too.

## Day 142 September 30, 1968

I got my SP/4 orders this morning. Got paid today $155.00. off this morning. Had to help Sgt. Beavers tear down a building. Then I had to help build a platform for all the spools of cable. Have K.P. tonight.

## Day 143 October 1, 1968

K.P. was a son-of-a-bitch last night. That damn cook had me doing all kinds of shit. I am off today, and I am tired as hell. Went to the PX and post office. Sent Jeannie $80.00. Ordered me a Nehru suit. Lost $15.00 at the club playing cards.

**Day 144 October 2, 1968**

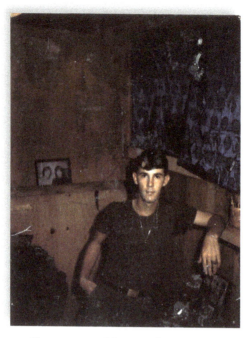

Had to pull motor stables in the motor pool. They assigned us guys in Cable Section trucks today. They gave me an A-27, which is dead lined. (don't run). After lunch I had to work up at the line shack. Had to put some boards on the platform, then fill a hole with sandbags. Went to the club tonight and had a couple of CC's. Sold my camera today to my grass buddy Jones for $75.00. Bought a radio and tape recorder from Sgt. Beavers.

**Day 145 October 3, 1968**

Had to go on sick call this morning because of an itch on my crotch. They gave me some suave for it. Went to the massage shop and took a steam bath and shower and got a massage. This afternoon me and Wilbert had to cut some weeds. Had to work from 6 to 7 because we didn't show up for revelry this morning. Saw some stag movies tonight for $2.00, boy they were sickening too.

**Day 146 October 4, 1968**

Right now I am drunk as a skunk. I made the man today. I had to go to the battalion to stand an inspection. They had a ⅔ alert. They had a ⅓ alert about 7:00, so I got off and went to the club and got drunk. Me and Wilbert had to sandbag the billets today. I was off this afternoon.

**Day 147 October 5, 1968**

I was off this morning because I made the man yesterday. This afternoon I had to go down to DTOC to tear a wall down, and fill sandbags. We had work call tonight, we had to cut grass at the com-center. I won $81.00 in poker tonight.

**Day 148 October 6, 1968**

I didn't get to sleep this morning. I had to go back over to the com-center to cut grass, but they gave me the afternoon off. I got a pass from the CO. Bought a couple of things. Everything was off limits, so if we would have got caught our shit would have been flaky. I bought a small tape recorder from Knittle for $27.00, so I'll send Jeannie my other one. Well I finally got a letter from my brother Frank today, the first in about four months. Won $30.00 in poker tonight.

**Day 149 October 7, 1968**

Had to drive a ¾ ton (A-26) today. Went to DTOC to fill sandbags. Didn't do too much work. Have to drive again tomorrow. A 2½ ton (A-54) won $40.00 in poker tonight.

**Day 150 October 8, 1968**

Today we had to pull motor stables on all the trucks. I had to drive an A-54 a 2 1/2 ton truck around. Didn't work at DTOC because they were having a meeting down there. Had to drive a couple of Sgt's to the P.X. won $30.00 in poker tonight.

## Day 151 October 9, 1968

I was on the trouble team today. Had to put in two lines at the com-center. Had to put in a phone at S-3. I had to fix the EM and NCO club lines. They had a show at the EM club tonight. It was a shity show, but the girls did look good, they were from Austria. After I got back from the club I had to go over to Favor and fix two phones at S-2 and S-5 had to replace the S-5 phone.

### Day 152 October 10, 1968
We had an alert this morning about 5:30. I got to sleep until 10:00 this morning, because I had to go out at 11:30 last night to Favor's to fix the C.O.'s line, but it was his switchboard. I worked until about 12:30. I had to go over to DTOC to fill some sandbags. Had to T.I. A-22. We mixed some cement today and made a patio. Won $60.00 in poker tonight.

### Day 153 October 11, 1968
Had to take a switchboard over to DTOC this morning. The division photographer took some pictures of us sitting it up. I was off this afternoon because I have guard on Dragon mountain tonight. SP/4 Luncan challenged me for the man, but he lost, so I won the man again today. I lost $5.00 in poker tonight.

### Day 154 October 12, 1968

Well they didn't have a ⅔ alert last night so I didn't have to pull guard duty. I slept all day because I felt bad from a cold. I brought a typewriter from Sgt Mohn tonight for $40.00. Mailed Jeannie's tape recorder to her today, which cost me $ 4.88 airmail.

### Day 155 October 13, 1968

We got to sleep in this morning. I started to go to church but I never did make it. I had to stay in the line shack all day, but the only good thing about it. I didn't do any work all day. Had a drink at the club tonight.

## Day 156 October 14, 1968

Today I had to help put a pole in, and then dig another hole and put another pole in it. I got to go to the P.X. This afternoon, then me and Jones had to go down to D.S.O. to get some lumber for the first Sgt. Worked out tonight with some weights and springs.

## Day 157 October 15, 1968

Had to go to the rifle range this morning. Had to go get some lumber at the 5th and 60th but they moved. So I came back to the company and played pool and listened to the radio. We had a shake down this evening. Me and Wilbert took some pictures in our same suits tonight.

**Day 158 October 16, 1968**

Had to go up to S-4 to get some gear I never received when I first got over here. This afternoon I had to help load some barbed wire on a truck and then take it to the dump. Then I had to go and help rewire the B&Q billets with Sgt Mohn & SP/4 Dalton. We worked until about 5:30 this evening.

## Day 159 October 17, 1968

Today we had to pull motor stables on our trucks. This afternoon I had to help load some lumber and throw it away. I am supposed to have K.P. tonight, but Sgt. Duncan is going to have someone replace me. So I can go on the sweep tomorrow.

## Day 160 October 18, 1968

Some of Cable section on Swe.

We had to get up at 3:00 this morning. We had a little trouble with Charlie today. They killed one of them and wounded another one, but he and two others got away. Other than that the sweep was all right. We had to go over another little creek that was pretty deep. We didn't get back until about 7:30 tonight. So today was the first day I really got to play G.I. Joe, and it was for real.

## Day 161 October 19, 1968

Me, Sgt Jones, Malloy, Dalton, Grantham, and Robinson had to go out to the tea plantation to help look for the three guys who got lost yesterday. They were from the 278th signal company. They were found by choppers this afternoon. All I did was play taxi driver with my ¾ ton. Me & Sgt Mohn had to go up to Fang to put in a 207 and wire it up. I got a pen pal today from Cincinnati, his name is Gary Godfred.

## Day 162 October 20, 1968

Today was a slow, wet, and windy day. We got to sleep in this morning. I went to church this morning, then when I got back I didn't do anything but go to sleep. This afternoon I had to help clean out the ditch around our billets. Sgt Duncan told me today I've got a good chance to make E-5 before I leave here. I have to go up to Fang tonight at 11:30 and help Sgt. Mohn put in a 207, and we're supposed to get off in the morning.

## Day 163 October 21, 1968

I got to sleep this morning, me & Sgt Mohn worked at Fang last night. We rewired a 207, I was off this morning. We had to exchange our MPC (money) today. I was off this afternoon because I have guard duty on Dragon Mountain tonight. Well I got screwed out of the man today, so that means that I'll have to pull guard duty tonight.

## Day 164 October 22, 1968

I had the first shift last night on guard 9–12. The wind was blowing hard but I didn't get cold. I slept from 12–6:30 which wasn't bad. I was off this morning. This afternoon I gave my ¾ ton a grease job. Then I washed all my field gear and boots. So really I didn't do much today. Had to T. I. my truck for trouble team tomorrow.

## Day 165 October 23, 1968

I was on trouble team all day. Had to work up at Fang and S-3 most of the day. Sgt Duncan helped me and SP/4 Luncan put a line to mars. The rest of the day wasn't too bad. The show at the club was pretty good tonight.

**Day 166 October 24, 1968**

They called us out last night about 10:00 and we had to stay out until 1:00. The line from bunker 129 was out. We never did fix it. They made me get up at 6:00 this morning, and boy it sure gave me the ass. I was on trouble team again today. Had to T.I. my truck this morning. This afternoon we only ran a line from Fang to Black building. I sure hope they don't call me out tonight.

**Day 167 October 25, 1968**

I was on trouble team again today. They didn't call us out last night. Didn't have too much trouble today. Only a few lines out. I bought a turntable, amp, and speakers tonight from Malloy for $200.00. We have an inspection tomorrow from the brass, so Sgt Duncan & Sgt Beavers came in and got us out of bed to clean up the billets. I don't have trouble team tomorrow, and I am glad.

**Day 168 October 26, 1968**

Today was a very good day, because I didn't do anything. All I did was go to the water point to help wash some trucks, but all I did was read a book, boy I got blown away on grass tonight, and was digging on the groovy sounds of the Beatles and Doors.

**Day 169 October 27, 1968**

Today has been another good day. I went to church this morning. Then I was off this afternoon for I have guard on the mountain tonight. Well I made the man again, so I am off tonight and tomorrow. I got blown away on pot tonight.

**Day 170 October 28, 1968**

I was off today for making the man yesterday. I slept until 12:00. This afternoon I went with SP/4 Malloy on the Vietnamese run. I got blown away on pot again tonight.

**Day 171 October 29, 1968**

We had an alert this morning. Today I had to drive the A-26. I had to help Sgt. Trabue rewire some J/1077 boxes this morning. This afternoon I helped him again. Washed the truck. Got blown away again tonight. They had a show, but we had another alert so the show left. I had to man the bunker in the motor pool during the alert this morning and tonight. I tore up all the letters my family and friends sent me. I also tore up Miss Jeannie Brownfields.

**Day 172 October 30, 1968**

Today I've been in the army for one year, so now I have two to go. Now I am a U.S. instead of a R.A. The first year has been a good experience for me. Today was a pretty good day. I had to T. I. A-26 to drive today. I messed up the gears. Me & Knittle had to build a lumber rack. Me & the boys got blown away again tonight. We even got Malloy nice with us. He wanted to go again. I sold my radio to Dean. Do you realize about 85% of this company are potheads. C company 95% and headquarters 90%.

**Day 173 October 31, 1968**

Today was a pretty good day. This morning we got paid. I drew $259.00 but I had to pay out $250.00. We didn't work this morning, and I was off this afternoon for I have guard tonight. But I made the man. I got blown away with Malloy & Wiggins tonight.

**Day 174 November 1, 1968**

I was off all day for making the man yesterday. Went to the PX, and got my suit. Got blown away again tonight. Lost all my money in poker tonight.

## Day 175 November 2, 1968

This morning I helped build a pole rack behind the line shack. Boy there's this good looking girl who comes over to the tailor shop, and she's out of this world. This afternoon I had to help Sgt. Beavers build a sidewalk in the company area. We had a shakedown this morning. We have to be in bed by 11:30 PM tonight, they have a curfew in the division. I didn't get blown away tonight, I got annihilated. All of this chicken shit is making me sick to my stomach, so I have to do something to forget all this shit so I get stoned on pot.

## Day 176 November 3, 1968

Today was a pretty good day. I had to go to the rifle range this morning. We didn't get to sleep this morning. We had another shakedown. Boy, I pulled a slick one at the range today, I got in the back of the truck and went to sleep. This afternoon I had to make some circuit charts for Sgt. Duncan. I won $10 in poker tonight. I didn't get nice tonight on pot. I got two letters from Jeannie telling me about my brother's party. My buddy Wilbert fell and cut his leg tonight, so he might miss his R&R in two days.

## Day 177 November 4, 1968

I had to go to the dentist this morning, but I have to go back tomorrow. All the work I did was finish those circuit charts. I went down to see Wilbert. I bought four albums today. I taped them this evening. We had another alert this morning, and I had to go to the bunkers. Well I got blown away tonight, and I mean blown away.

## Day 178 November 5, 1968

I fell asleep on Wilbert's bed last night and didn't wake up until this morning. We had to pull motor stables this morning. I went back to the dentist this afternoon but I was late, so I have to go back in the morning. I didn't do any work this afternoon. Got blown away tonight. Got a tape from mom and family and Jeannie tonight.

## Day 179 November 6, 1968

I went to the dentist this morning and got a tooth filled. I had K.P. (kitchen police) the rest of the day and it was a bitch, I hate K.P. I got blown away again tonight.

## Day 180 November 7, 1968

Today I got two more teeth filled, and boy I thought that dentist was going to kill me. My face was hurting all day long. I worked in the line shack this afternoon.

We have a sweep tomorrow. I didn't get high on the pot tonight.

**Day 181 November 8, 1968**
We had to go on a sweep today, and it was hot as hell. We didn't walk too far, but it was so hot, it seemed like it was a hundred miles. One of our trucks ran over a mine. We didn't see any charlies today, thank God. The only hard thing about the sweep was it was hot as hell.

**Day 182 November 9, 1968**
We got to sleep an extra hour this morning. I was supposed to put a window on a jeep today, but we didn't have any hinges. I went to the dentist again today and got another tooth filled. I only have my front one to fill now. I have to go back on Monday. Didn't do anything this afternoon.

**Day 183 November 10, 1968**
We got to sleep in this morning. I went to church. After church I had to work in the motor pool. I was off this afternoon because I have guard on the bunker line. I had a lot of competition for the man from Brown, Luncan, and Grantham, all of these guys have made the man before. Well I beat all of them for the man.

One of the guys, Luncan, got sick on the bunker line tonight, so I have to go and pull guard for him, boy have I got the ass. They think he has Malaria, but I am still off all day tomorrow.

**Day 184 November 11, 1968**

I was off today for making the man yesterday. I sold my AMP and recorder to Robinson for $250.00 today. I got my new glasses today. I got a little nice tonight on pot. I think I will get a pass tomorrow.

**Day 185 November 12, 1968**

Today was a pretty good day. This morning we had to pull motor stables. I got a pass this afternoon and went to Pleiku. I bought my darling Jeannie a sweater, and I got a walking cane also. We had to work tonight until 8:00 PM which gave me the ass. I am supposed to drive the Labor run tomorrow, but I am going to the dentist.

**Day 186 November 13, 1968**

Had to work on the deadline trucks this morning. Went and got the rest of my teeth filled today. Worked on A-53 when I got back. We had to work in the motor pool this evening. They are having patrols every other day now starting today, and boy that is a bunch of shit. I got Jeannie's package today and enjoyed it very much.

**Day 187 November 14, 1968**

Today was a pretty good day. This morning I had to pull motor stables. This afternoon I had to T.I. (truck inspection) a truck. Me, Malloy and Sgt. Duncan had to go out and pick up the patrol, but they were already gone. There were mines in the roadways but we didn't hit any.

**Day 188 November 15, 1968**

Today I had to drive the A-26 around looking for errors. I had to change a flat this morning. This afternoon me and Sgt. Duncan had to change duels on a deuce and a half. Then I just messed around in the motor pool the rest of the afternoon. I had to T.I. A-26 tonight for I have to drive it tomorrow. We have an inspection tomorrow. I fixed a writing table up tonight.

**Day 189 November 16, 1968**

I had to drive the A-26 again today, all I did was drive people to different places. The first platoon had a party tonight. I drank a couple of beers. Then I went out with Malloy, Jones, & Grantham and got wrecked on pot. They were bringing smoke on Charlies tonight outside the wire with choppers and spooky (ac-130 with mini gun).

**Day 190 November 17, 1968**

I had to T. I A-26 this morning after we got up. We got to sleep this morning, then I went to church. After church we just rode around in the truck. This afternoon I went over to DTOC & Favor, then just drove around. Had to T. I. A-26 again tonight. Got a tape from Jeannie today and I didn't like it at all. All she talked about is buying things.

**Day 191 November 18, 1968**

Well I got blown away last night after I wrote in my diary. Today, Me, Malloy, Knittle, and Sgt. Carter had to take some cable down. While we were out there Me, Knittle & Malloy got wrecked. I had to climb a pole. I had to drop from the lines and boy it was a long fall, it hurt my legs. I taped Jeannie tonight and told her she had to choose between me and her piggy girl friends. I won $40.00 in poker tonight.

**Day 192 November 19, 1968**

We had motor stables this morning, I helped pull them on A-22. Then I went to help police up wire from yesterday, then some more after lunch. This afternoon I went to the post office and P.X., and then sat around and read a book. I got another package from my darling Jeannie. I got really wrecked tonight.

**Day 193 November 20, 1968**

I went on sick call this morning. I have a pulled muscle in my right leg. I was off this afternoon, because I have guard duty on the mountain tonight. I beat Carson out for the man today. I am getting the ass at Miss Jeannie Brownfield, because she isn't writing to me as much as she should. If she keeps screwing around with me I am going to have to break our engagement up.

**Day 194 November 21, 1968**

I was off today. So I slept late and then read my book. The rest of the day I cleaned up my area. We had to clean our weapons tonight. We had a show at the EM club but I didn't stay over there. I went and got wrecked tonight, then I went for a second time, and boy was I wrecked.

**Day 195 November 22, 1968**

Today I was still feeling good from last night. I helped straighten up around the line shack. This afternoon I helped lay a diagram for the Ivy Bowl, where the Bob

Hope show is going to be. I had to go see the C.O. (commanding officer) tonight. I had ammo in my pockets and he offered me an article-15 or work for him for a week. I chose to work for him for a week. Some son-of-a-bitch burnt Jeannie's picture today, so I stopped all card playing at my table. I wrote her another shity letter tonight, and I might get some results from it.

### Day 196 November 23, 1968

Today I had to help dig a ditch over at the Ivy bowl. We're putting in the P.A. System for the Bob Hope show next month. Me and John had to work for the 1st Sgt. tonight from 6:00 until after dark. We have to eat chow at 4:30 AM tomorrow and be over at the bowl at 5:00 AM. Me, Malloy, and Jones got wrecked today.

### Day 197 November 24, 1968

Went to church this morning, afterwards I helped dig the ditches over at the Ivy Bowl. This afternoon I had to help fill sandbags around the wire billets, Me, Malloy, and Jones road around before lunch and got wrecked. I had to work for the 1st Sgt. tonight for two hours. I am going before the soldier of the month tomorrow. I sure hope I make it, it helps on the E-5 board.

**Day 198 November 25, 1968**

I had this afternoon off to get ready to go before the board of the soldier of the month, well I didn't get it, but no big deal. I was even glad to go and represent my company. This afternoon I had to help put tar on the sandbags around the wire billets, Boy I got that shit all over me too. I had to work for the 1st Sgt. again tonight. Knittle helped me tonight. Knittle, Grantham, and I went and got wrecked, then we went to the movie over at 278th signal bat. I am wrecked right now while I am writing this.

**Day 199 November 26, 1968**

We had motor stables this morning. I had to T. I A-2 a jeep, and then drive Lt. Long around for a while, when you get a job like this you've got it licked. I got wrecked tonight riding around in the jeep. I worked for the Sgt. again tonight, and had to cut some grass.

**Day 200 November 27, 1968**

I had to T. I. A-2 this morning and drive lt. Long and Sgt. Duncan around. This sure is a good job. John and I washed the jeep. Me and him rode around and got wrecked on pot. I got wrecked again tonight with

Malloy, Jones, and John riding around in a ¾ ton truck. Had to pull weeds out of the ditches in the company area for the 1st Sgt. Tonight, tomorrow is thanksgiving.

**Day 201 November 28, 1968**

Today was Thanksgiving and it was a nice one. I was billets orderly this morning. We had a one star general come around and check the place out. We had a very good dinner. I laid down about 3 today and didn't get back up until about 6. Then I had to go and work for the 1st Sgt. I got a package from my sweet dear mother today. It had a book, some smokes, and candy. I got double wrecked tonight with Harvey and Arther and I am reading the book mom sent me and it answers a lot of questions for me.

**Day 202 November 29, 1968**

We got paid this morning, I drew $239.00. I played cards. This morning I won about $30.00 and $10.00 tonight. Our main and only big PX burned down last night. I went up on VHF Hill this afternoon, but I didn't do anything. I had to work on my last night for the 1st Sgt. & got wrecked again tonight on pot.

## Day 203 November 30, 1968

Went over to the Ivy Bowl and helped put in the rest of the circuits for the P.A. system. I was off this afternoon because I have guard duty tonight. There were six guys who tried to beat me, but I beat them all for the man. I got wrecked again tonight with Malloy, and Jones. I am off all day tomorrow.

## Day 204 December 1, 1968

I was off all day. I got up at about 10:30. This afternoon I went to Camp Schsmit P.X. and bought a couple of things. I bought my love Jeannie a necklace. This afternoon I went with Wilbert and some of the other guys downtown. On the way back me and the guys blew a jay each. Then I went out with the boys and got wrecked some more on pot. They had a big shootout downtown while we were there.

**Day 205 December 2, 1968**

I had to clean cable all day, to get it ready to turn into salvage. We blew a joint this morning while we were working. I blew one joint tonight, but it wasn't enough to bother me. I am going to quit smoking this shit before it does something to me. They had a show tonight at the EM club, it wasn't bad.

**Day 206 December 3, 1968**

Right now I am writing with candle light, for we don't have any power. We saw some more stag movies tonight, and boy they sure make a fellow home sick for the girl he loves, or for that matter, any American girl. This morning we had to pull ESC on all of our trucks. This afternoon I had to clean some more cable. I have K.P. tomorrow.

**Day 207 December 4, 1968**

Today I had K.P. I went on the ration run this morning. This afternoon I read a very good book, Hot pursuit. I had to clean up the NCO side of the mess hall this evening. I lied, I got wrecked tonight.

## Day 208 December 5, 1968

This morning we had to pull motor stables. Me and Dalton pulled them on A-26 (¾ ton). I didn't do anything else the rest of the morning. This afternoon I had to drive the A-2 (jeep). I didn't do any work at all. I went to the show at the EM club tonight. I bought a camera from Dalton for $55.00. Got a shitty letter from Jeannie today.

**Day 209 December 6, 1968**

This morning I had to T. I. A-2 and drive Lt. Lewis around. I didn't do any work at all today. Only drove the jeep around the division. I got wrecked tonight on pot with some of the guys. We had a practice alert this morning.

**Day 210 December 7, 1968**

This morning I had to go out to DTOC and help put up a cable for the dial system phones. Me and Wilbert, Harvy and Aurther went out in the truck and got wrecked. After lunch we went back down to DTOC and finished putting up the cable. We got off at 3:00 today, for the Donut Dollies were at the mess hall this afternoon. They called a ⅔'s alert tonight.

## Day 211 December 8, 1968

We got to sleep this morning, and when I got up I went to church. They spotted 45 Charlies outside the wire last night. This afternoon I helped rewind some wire, but really I didn't do any work all day. I have guard duty tonight, but I got Wiggins to take my place so I can go on the sweep tomorrow, but I came to find out we aren't going to have one. Won $27.00 in cards tonight.

## Day 212 December 9, 1968

We had a shakedown this morning for a lost radio. I had to change a flat on A-25 (¾ ton) this morning.

It took me about an hour to do. This morning I had to drive a trouble team with Sgt. Carter. We went out on one job, but we didn't have to do any work. Me and Sgt. Duncan went to special services, and found out Bob Hope wasn't coming. After all that work we did for the show was a waste. I have guard duty tonight because we didn't have the sweep. I made the man with no problem, Me, Wilbert, Harvey, and Jones got wrecked tonight.

**Day 213 December 10, 1968**
Well today I slept until about 11:00. This afternoon I put some coppertone on and messed around in the sun trying to get a tan. I was off all day because I made the man again yesterday.

**Day 214 December 11, 1968**
Today was a very good day. I didn't do any work at all, just drove the jeep around. We got a new C.O. today. His name is Capt. Mason. Boy I had a hard time getting to sleep last night, I couldn't help thinking of R&R. They had work call tonight, but me and Sgt. Mohn went over to the Red Cross. I sent Jeannie another tape tonight.

## Day 215 December 12, 1968

Today was another good day. I drove the jeep for Lt. Lewis. We had to pull motor stables this morning. I ran all over hell and back today. This evening I drove Wiggins down for special services, and then me and him blew one joint apiece. They've started this shit called fire guard, which I think is a bunch of bull shit. Each guy has to pull 2 hour shifts. (just like in basic training).

## Day 216 December 13, 1968

Today was a good day, for I drove the jeep again. It wasn't as good as the other two days for I didn't do that much driving. Me and Harvey went out in the jeep and had one bowl of pot. We have an inspection tomorrow, but I am not worried about it.

## Day 217 December 14, 1968

Today was a very good day. I didn't do any work at all. I was barrack orderly all day long, but like always the dudes didn't have any inspection. This afternoon I played a little basketball. Me and some of the guys played some monopoly and I beat the shit out of them. I didn't smoke any pot tonight. I wrote Jeannie a letter tonight for the first time since I can remember, and not having one to answer I guess it's because I love her so much.

**Day 218 December 15, 1968**

We slept this morning. I went to church. The only thing I got against going to church is Mr. Latham preaching his opinion of things and not the Bible. For some odd reason I got a pass today with Grantham. I'm on fire guard tonight at 3:00 AM. I ordered a walking suit and a new suit today while I was downtown for $88.00.

**Day 219 December 16, 1968**

I had to help build some shelves in the line shack this morning. I was off this afternoon because I have guard on the mountain tonight. I didn't make the man today for the first time in about two months. John beat me because I didn't have enough ammo in my magazines. I have to pull guard on the mountain. Today I've been engaged for one year to Miss Jeannie Brownfield and I still love her very much.

## Day 220 December 17, 1968

Guard wasn't bad last night. I had it from 3:00 AM until 6:00 AM but I went to sleep about 4:30 AM until 6:30 AM. I was off this morning. I drove the jeep this afternoon. We have a sweep tomorrow. So if anything happens to me let it be known that I loved Jeannie Brownfield and her only.

## Day 221 December 18, 1968

I was supposed to go on the sweep today, but I had to go to Qui Nhon to pick up some new 2½ ton trucks. I didn't leave until 1:15 on a C-130 plane. I left my shades (sunglasses) at the airport in Pleiku. We got to Qui Nhon about 2:00 PM. We finally got to where we were going to stay. I went downtown and had a couple of drinks. Jones brought 39 joints. They had a show at the EM NCO club and me and Arther drank one bourbon and coke.

## Day 222 December 19, 1968

We went and picked up our new 2 1/2 this morning. Me and Arther slept in this morning, and some second lieutenant had the ass. We finally got back to Camp Grantic, but it was too late to go downtown. We also had to pick up three crates of sandbags for each truck. Me and Auther just sat around and bullshitted about our girl friends the rest of the night. We're supposed to go back to Pleiku tomorrow.

**Day 223 December 20, 1968**

Well we didn't leave today, because we didn't have any gunships to go with us. We had to stay at 669 th Trans Company overnight. There wasn't much to do down here. They had a pretty good show at the club tonight.

**Day 224 December 21, 1968**

We left for Pleiku about 7:30 AM this morning and got here about 11:30 AM. The drive back was alright. We had a little rain outside of Qui Nhon. I smoked 11 j's on the way back, which didn't bother me at all, except make my eyes burn. We had to wait around until about 4:30

to get our trucks unloaded. Boy you should have seen my beard, it was long. We had a party at the line shack tonight, but I left and got wrecked on pot. Sgt. Duncan knows we smoke. He found out for sure last night.

**Day 225 December 22, 1968**

We didn't get to sleep this morning because of that MedCap village shit. I didn't go to church this morning because I helped Sgt. Duncan built a room all day in the line shack. I got a package from Jeannie today. The Vodka was broken so I don't think I'll be able to celebrate Christmas. Anne sent me a Christmas card today. I have to go out to the MedCap village tomorrow and work.

**Day 226 December 23, 1968**

Today was the only day that I've worked over here that I've felt I've done something worthwhile. I helped the Montagnard people move their things. A 2 ½ ton truck hit my ¾ ton truck this afternoon. I had to fill out an accident report, and I have to see the C.O. tonight. The accident couldn't be avoided, I had John and two of the village women with me, nobody was hurt. The right side of A-22 was caved in. I got wrecked this afternoon. Robinson smoked with us today, his first time. Everyone in this cable section either smokes or has smoked before.

## Day 227 December 24, 1968

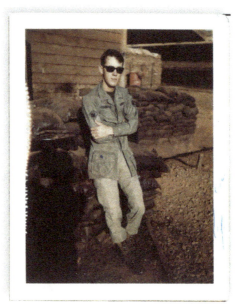

I had to help Sgt Duncan put in a plug in the mess hall, then I helped him a little by working on his room. I was supposed to be on guard tomorrow, but I took Jogerson's place today. I made the man. I bought two quarts of 100 Pipers, (whiskey) but I didn't drink any. The guys drank one of the quarts. I am off all day tomorrow, which is Christmas. Happy Birthday, Jesus. I wish all my friends and family and the girl I love Jeannie a very merry Christmas.

**Day 228 December 25, 1968)**

Today was Christmas. I was off all day because I made the man yesterday. I got up at about 9:00 this morning. We had a very good dinner. I went to sleep this afternoon and then watched the army/navy game which was won by the army 21–14. Then I took a shower, and then I went to the show at the EM club. They had a little trouble after the show. Some guy from 278th was cut. I took him to 4th med in the trouble team truck. So I want to wish everybody back home a very Merry Christmas.

**Day 229 December 26, 1968**

We had to pull motor stables this morning. I helped Auther Jones pull them on A-2 the jeep. This afternoon I didn't do anything, but sham. I went out with Malloy, Davis, Grantham, and McDowell in the 2 ½ and got wrecked on pot. We had a work call tonight. We had to clean our weapon (M-16) and our gas mask. I really cleaned my weapon. It isn't too long until R&R and beautiful Hawaii.

**Day 230 December 27, 1968**

This morning, I had to dig some holes to put some poles in. This afternoon I helped put in the poles. John fell and one of the poles rolled over her right hand, and I had to lift it off of him, and boy it sure was heavy. Then I helped Sgt. Duncan clean up the line shack. We had a 1800 (6:00 PM) formation, we had to check all of our fire equipment. I got wrecked with Conklin and Link tonight under a blanket so the M.P.'s couldn't see us smoking.

### Day 231 December 28, 1968

I was supposed to have K.P. today, but me and McDowell traded. I have his guard duty tomorrow. I didn't do much work today. I helped Sgt. Mohn build a gun rack. I spent most of the day painting my picture. I got wrecked tonight, and I really mean wrecked.

### Day 232 December 29, 1968

I shamed all morning. I was still feeling good from last night, and then I went out with Jones and smoked a jay and it made me wrecked. I didn't do any work at all this morning. I have guard this afternoon. I was so wrecked I couldn't hardly get ready, John and Ed helped me clean my weapon and shine my boots. I made the man because I had the cleanest weapon. I was wrecked when I did it too. I went out with the boys tonight and got double wrecked.

## Day 233 December 30, 1968

I was off all day today, because I made the man yesterday. I got up about 10:00 this morning, and cleaned my room. I just laid around the rest of the day doing nothing. I went out with some of the guys tonight on the hill and got wrecked on pot. Sgt Jenning was there, and he's new to me. The C.O. gave us an inspection on our M-17's and M-1 tonight. I have to go to the village tomorrow with Smith and Wilbert.

## Day 234 December 31, 1968

Today is the last day of 1968. I had to work at the village again this morning. I just drove a ¾ ton to haul wood for the villagers, we only worked half a day. I was off the rest of the afternoon. They had a party at the mess hall but it was nothing. I went out with Arther and Harvey and got wrecked. I won about $40.00 playing cards tonight. I have $470.00 for R&R. Well this has been a prosperous year, let's hope the following are as good. It was a good year.

## Day 235 (January 1, 1969

Happy new year. I sat up last night and watched the new year come in. I was also wrecked. Only one good thing happened today and that was, we got to sleep this morning. I didn't do anything this morning. This afternoon Wilbert and I went to get our shots. They weren't giving them today. Then I went to the P.X. Sgt. Duncan put me on fire guard tonight. I bought myself another camera today for $100.00, and sold mine for $50.00. Happy New Year family and Jeannie.

### Day 236 January 2, 1969

This morning we had motor stables. I pulled them on A-26. Won $40.00 on the Rose Bowl with Ohio St. won ten on the Orange Bowl on Penn. St. Won $90.00 in cards tonight. Had guard today, and I made the man again. They had two men today, so me and Carson made it. I am off all day tomorrow. 4 days left until beautiful Hawaii.

### Day 237 January 3, 1969

Today was a pretty good day. I was off all day for making the man yesterday. I got up and cleaned my room. I had to go down and get three shots for R&R Monday, Sgt Buchanan made me a team chief tonight. So as of tomorrow I am in charge of 4 men. Tomorrow is my last working day until after R&R. I got a wonderful tape from home today, it was taped on Christmas day.

**Day 238 January 4, 1969**

Well for some odd reason it rained today, and all day. I had to drive a ¾, A-26 to police up wire with Sgt. Halloy and SP/4 Grantham. I climbed on a pole and it was one of those big ones. I went out and got wrecked tonight. I am off tomorrow to get all my things ready for R&R. Sgt. Suttle needs a room, so they are giving him Sgt. Carter's so that means I have to get out.

**Day 239 January 5, 1969**

Today was a very good day, I was off all day. We got to sleep in this morning. I got my orders signed, and baggage checked, but they didn't even check it. Then I went to sleep, and then watched a football game. Went to see a good movie at 278th. The green beret was on. I leave for Hawaii tomorrow.

**Day 240 January 6, 1969**

Today was one day I didn't mind getting up. I left for R&R this morning. We got to the airport about 6:30 AM this morning, and didn't get to leave until 4:30 this afternoon. I bought myself a good watch today. Then Me, Wilbert and some guy named Harris went downtown Pleiku. I just bought a pair of shades. When we got back our plane was ready to leave. We got here in Cam Rahn about 5:30. Right now I am getting ready to go to bed. We process out tomorrow, and leave the 8th. Boy it was a very long and slow day.

**Day 241 January 7, 1969**

Well today was another slow day. The PX's down here didn't have anything I wanted. We went over to the air force PX, and they didn't have anything either. My buddies, Harvey and Boone got down here today. We had a jay tonight and boy I mean it really tasted good.

I bought myself a new wallet today. I got an engraving on my watch today that says Kenny loves Jeannie. I processed out in the morning at 7:00, and I also changed my money over to American money.

## Day 242 January 8, 1969

This morning I didn't mind getting up at all. I am on a Pan American airline right now at 12:50 PM. I changed my money over and processed out this morning, so when I get to Hawaii it will be the 8th again, so I'll have to save some space for the second 8th of January. We got to Hawaii about 5:00 this morning. I called mom. Me and Wilbert bought some clothes. I bought about $80.00 worth. I called the one I love, Jeannie today. Boy my legs sure are tired from walking so much today. I had a date with Linda Perkins tonight, but she was a weirdo, so I told her to hit the road. My hotel cost me $72.00 for six days.

## Day 243 January 9, 1969

I did a lot of walking again today. It rained all day long. Wilbert rented a car so me and him and Stean went to sears. I went to the Lemon Tree tonight, but there wasn't anybody there but couples so I left. Then a taxi took me to the hotel street, but the pigs in that bar turned my stomach. Then I came home and went to bed. So for this R&R isn't worth shit.

**Day 244 January 10, 1969**

Today we finally had some sunshine and I took advantage of it. I laid on the beach all day long. I met a girl named Mary, and boy she's what was happening. She's a head from way back. I had a very good time with her on the beach. I went to see her at work tonight and had a drink. She works at Georgia's Inn. I am supposed to go over to her apartment in the morning. She's Italian. I went to the lemon tree again tonight and that place has about had it. There's nothing to do around this place and women are hard to find.

**Day 245 January 11, 1969**

I got up this morning and went to the beach and waited for Mary. She finally came, and we laid in the sun, and then went in the water for about five minutes. She fed me some lunch this afternoon. Me, Wilbert, and Stean went to the beach and took some movies. I went to Georgie's Inn tonight about 8:00, and stayed there until Mary got off, which was 2:00, and then she, Wilbert, Stean and myself had a couple of drinks, and took a couple of pictures.

## Day 246 January 12, 1969

Well, today I got up and watched the fourth quarter of the Super Bowl which the colts lost 16–7. Then I went to the beach, but Mary didn't come down, so I went to her house. While I was there she was making a blouse. She gave me a pill and I've felt great all day long. While I was wrecked I went to the beach and wrote some poems. I think they were pretty. Me and Mary went out tonight, but we only walked around and goofed on the scenery. I called Jeannie yesterday. I have to leave tomorrow night at 12:00. I got drunk last night and tonight and I was really gone with the pill.

# Day 247 January 13, 1969

Today, I got up at 9:00 and went to Mary's house, to tell her goodbye. Me, Wibert and Stean went to the airport just to see how to get there. I drove, and boy believe me it really felt good to drive an American car. I just drove around all day long taking pictures. I called Jeannie again today to tell her and everybody else goodbye. I really hate to go back tonight, but I know I have to, so it isn't a big thing.

### Day 248 January 14, 1969

I left Hawaii last night at about 1:30. So on this day I didn't do anything but sleep. I woke up twice to eat some food. All the other times I was sleeping so on this day I didn't do anything at all.

### Day 249 January 15, 1969

We arrived in Cam Ranh Bay about 9:30 this morning. We had our money changed over and got our tickets for our flight back to Pleiku tomorrow. I went to sleep today and woke up at about 2:00, went and ate some chow, and then I tried to read some comics, but I was too sleepy and tired so I went back to sleep.

### Day 250 January 16, 1969

I got up at a quarter till seven in the morning. Caught a bus to the airport where I waited about an hour for our plane. We got to Pleiku about 9:30 this morning, and came back to our company. All I did today was try and straighten up some of my junk. I hated like hell to come back to this place, but here, I am again where the shit flies thick. I really hate this place. Arther took me out and got me wrecked this afternoon.

**Day 251 January 17, 1969**

Well today, I was in charge of four guys who had to go out and police up loose and bad wire. Me and Link smoked a couple of jays this afternoon. I climbed one pole and I was wrecked when I did it. So it was a pretty good day. We didn't have any lifers with us to tell us what to do. We got them all policed up. We went to the movie in the jeep. I have fireguard tonight from 3:00 until 5:30.

**Day 252 January 18, 1967**

I was on the same job today with Link, Robinson and Smith. We finished by the 1st building. I had to climb upon a ladder and tape the wires together. I also got wrecked this morning before lunch. They sent a Sgt. with us this afternoon and we didn't get shit done. He was the new one we got a couple of days ago. I wrote about ten letters tonight, and I still have more to write. Tonight is the first time I haven't smoked, since I've been back from Hawaii. I slept during fireguard last night.

**Day 253 January 19, 1969**

This morning I had to go get A-54 a duece ½ out of the motor pool and drive it up to the lower part of Dragon mt. There we had to run a spiral 4 cable. Well I was supposed to have guard duty tonight, but I made the man again. I rode around with Link and got wrecked. Then Me and Knittle rode around in A-2 because I had to turn it in. We smoked a bowl and got wrecked better. I am off tomorrow, I am going to try and go downtown.

**Day 254 January 20, 1969**

I was off all day today because I made the man again yesterday. This morning I straightened up my lockers and put some things in my duffle bag. This afternoon, I got a pass to downtown Pleiku. I got my walking suit and paid my Nahru off. I didn't like my walking suit. I went out with Link and Grantham tonight in the jeep and got wrecked.

**Day 255 January 21, 1969**

I had to T. I A-25 this morning. Then I had to drive the trouble team truck. I didn't do any work this morning with the team. General McAlister came today and presented our mess hall with a plague for being the best mess hall in the division for the month of December.

This afternoon I helped Sgt. Duncan put some stakes for a place to wash our trucks. Then I had to take a phone up on VHF hill and test a four spiral cable. We had motor stables tonight at 6:00. I didn't have to do anything because I am a team chief, and as long as I don't have to do any shit like that, I like it.

**Day 256 January 22, 1969**

Well I didn't do anything this morning but sat around the line shack. This afternoon, I helped Sgt. Duncan dig some large holes. A buddy of mine came over today. He's with the 8th infantry. His name is Barth or Snoopy. Went out with him tonight and got wrecked. That was Me, Wilbert, Link, and Barth, I am wrecked right now and lying here listening to Jefferson airplane. They made me a guard today over a guy named Guynn.

**Day 257 January 23, 1969**

Well today, I didn't do anything except guard Guynn. We played pool this morning. This afternoon we played some cards. This is a very good job I've got. All I have to do is guard him,we're supposed to leave for Long Bihn tomorrow, but I don't know for sure. I have to wear a 45 with me all the time while I am guarding him. I just realized today that Miss Brownfield has only written me two letters this whole month. I sent my mom my film from Hawaii tonight.

**Day 258 January 24, 1969**

Sgt. Buchanan, Guynn and myself left for Long Bihn today. We had a little trouble getting there. First, we missed our flight this morning. Then we had to go to the Pleiku air base and catch a flight to Cam Ranh Bay. When we got to Cam Ranh Bay we caught another flight to Saigon, that's where we are now. I am standing guard over Guynn while he's locked up in a Conex. Buchanan is supposed to relieve me sometime tonight, but I don't know when. We should be able to get too Long Bihn in the morning. We also have to take a prisoner back with us when we go back.

**Day 259 January 25, 1969**

We had to sleep on the ground last night for about four hours. We took Guynn to L.B.J. this morning. The M.P. 's and Buchanan was inside, so I just rode around in Saigon. Then, they took me to the airport in Saigon, where I went to sleep. Buchanan came about 2:30. He had the guy who we were supposed to take back with us, his name is Frank. We flew to Cam Ranh Bay and got a flight in the morning to Pleiku. We went to a movie tonight, and then just walked around. Saigon has a lot of American cars in it and it reminded me of the states.

**Day 260 January 26, 1969**

We left Cam Ranh Bay this morning and arrived in Pleiku about 10:00. We took the guy Frank to his company. I bought myself a suitcase yesterday at the PX. I was off all day and I just sat around and wrote letters and played cards. I went out with Mullins. Tony, and Lapping, when I got back today. Then I went out with Link and got wrecked again. So it seems every time I go somewhere I get wrecked when I get back.

**Day 261 January 27, 1969**

This morning I had to cut some logs 10 feet long, then I had to cut some more 15 feet long. This afternoon, I got wrecked with Mullins, and Knittle, then I had to help Molloy & Mullins put up a power cable. Then I went out with Conklin and got wrecked again. We went to the show over at the Ivy Bowl. Then Me, Link, Grantham, Conklin and John went out again, then I came back and tried to tape Jeannie, but I couldn't finish it because I was wrecked. I have K.P tomorrow.

**Day 262 January 28, 1969**

Today I had K.P. which I didn't do too much all day long. The only time you really have to work is after the Vietnamese helpers leave. Then you have to do what they were doing. I had to wash the pots and pans. I went over to Favor and smoked two jays. Tonight I went over to the show and then Me, Link, and John went out and had four jays, and right now I am wrecked.

**Day 263 January 29, 1969**

This morning I drove the jeep A-2. They found two jays in it this morning, and one in the C.O's jeep. I drove Sgt. Duncan to Finance, and then Lt. Lewis made his rounds. I have guard duty this afternoon, but I made the man again. I went out with Conklin in A-65 and got wrecked, then I went to sleep in Wilbert's bed and didn't get up until about 10:30. I got my two other rolls of film back today.

**Day 264 January 30, 1969**

I was off all day for making the man yesterday. I woke up about 8:00 this morning and wrote to Jeannie, then I went back to sleep until 12:00, then I got up and ate chow. I just sat around the rest of the day and played cards. I went out with Link, Knittle & Grantham tonight and got wrecked on pot. We went to the show and we pulled up right beside an M.P. and he searched the shit out of us, but found nothing. Starting tomorrow I only have 100 days left.

### Day 265 January 31, 1969

This morning we got paid. I drew $238.00. Then me and Wilbert, Malloy and Lapping had to load some burnt wire on a 2 1/2 ton. This afternoon, Wilbert and Holly had to go downtown Pleiku where Johnson and some other guys were working and pick up some lumber. We fixed the truck to where it wouldn't start, so we could stay down there for the night. I went downtown Pleiku. I was driving downtown in a jeep where it was off limits. I smoked 3 jays and 4 bowls.

### Day 266 February 1, 1969

Yesterday was the best day I've spent over here. When we got back this morning we stopped by and I bought a pack of jays for $3.00. This was the second time I've paid for any since I've been smoking. Sgt Mohn and Sgt Ivey had the ass this morning, but there wasn't a damn thing they could do about it. We just screwed all over these damn lifers. This afternoon I had to unload the truck and then put some sandbags in it. I have to guard three prisoners and help escort them to Long Binh. I lost $20.00 in poker, tonight me and Link went out and got wrecked tonight. This was the worst I've ever been wrecked.

## Day 267 February 2, 1969

I was so wrecked last night I couldn't even write my diary for yesterday. I had to write it this morning. I received a letter from Jeannie yesterday, and because it was so short I read it, and tore it up without answering it. We got to sleep in this morning. Then I had to guard three prisoners all day long. Mims,Baxter and Jilterson. They had to help build a wall around our billets. Me, Link, Knittle, and John went out in the jeep and got wrecked.

## Day 268 February 3, 1969

I woke up this morning at 4:00 AM with my stomach hurting. I threw up when I got up this morning. This is the first time I've ever gotten sick since I've been here. I had to go to the 4th med, they sent me to the 71st EVAC, they put me through a lot of changes. They still don't know what's wrong with me, I have to go back the 19th and stay all night, and then get some more x-rays. I didn't get wrecked tonight, because nobody has any stuff. I am confined to base camp until I get my x-rays, which means I don't have to go on sweeps and patrols.

## Day 269 February 4, 1969

I had to guard the prisoners again all day. This one dude named Mims is nuts. He is always throwing things. I thought I was going to have to shoot him a couple of times today. He gave Lt. Lewis, the 1st Sgt and the C.O. Capt. Mason, a hard time. This is a bitch of a job guarding three. They have a sweep tomorrow, but I can't go because I have to guard these guys. I went out with Conklin tonight and got wrecked.

**Day 270 February 5, 1969**

The C. Q. runner came and got me about 11:30 last night and told me I had to stay all night with the prisoners. Another prisoner came in, which made four. Prisoners had to carry out lumber all day today. My company had a sweep today, which didn't last too long. They got back about 3:00 today. These guys, Baxter, Mims, Tilterson and Brick have to leave tomorrow and boy, am I glad, they have run me to death I went out with McDowell and Knittle tonight and got wrecked.

**Day 271 February 6, 1969**

They had a little trouble with Mims this morning. He kicked Lt. Lewis's ass. They put him in a straight jacket the rest of the day. They didn't have to work today, they just sat around in the day room all day. We had to take them up to Battalion this evening, and on the way me and two of the prisoners, Baxter and Tilterson and Link had a couple of jays on the way up. Then Me, Grantham, and Link went to the NCO club and had a drink before we went out in the jeep and got wrecked, Robinson went with us too. John mailed my 15 rolls of film today.

## Day 272 February 7, 1969

We didn't leave again today, but we are supposed to leave tomorrow for sure. We had to go to a General court-Martial for Mims this afternoon, it lasted about four hours. They haven't decided on what to do with him yet. Boy this weather is something else over here, when you have to sleep in long johns here in Vietnam. It really gets cold in the night and early morning. Me & Link went out in the jeep and got wrecked tonight and we saw lots of M.P.'s. Tomorrow is Jeannie's birthday.

## Day 273 February 8, 1969

Today is Jeannie's birthday, happy birthday love. Well we didn't leave again today, so we'll leave tomorrow. The

1st Sgt made the guys work this afternoon and then we went to the mess hall to play games with the Red Cross girls. Mims had to leave this morning. Sgt Ball took him down. His was the only order that came down from Battalion. Me, Link, Conklin, and Grantham went over to the service club and got wrecked. I beat Link in 4 games to none in Ping Pong, then went out in the jeep and got wrecked again. Happy birthday Jeannie.

### Day 274 February 9, 1969
Well we finally left today. Me, Jennings, Baxter and Tilterson went to Saigon. We all got wrecked this morning on the way to the Pleiku airport. We got to Saigon and then we had to go to MACV. H.Q. and waited on a bus to take us to Long Birch Jail, we turned the prisoners in and then went and got something to eat. Then Sgt. Ball came down and got us, we are staying at the 1st signal battalion. I had the best shower that can be had over here tonight. The showers are really nice. Me, Jennings, Ball and his brother went to a floor show and then watched a movie. We're going to Saigon tomorrow.

### Day 275 February 10, 1969
Me, Jennings, Ball and his brother and some other guys went to Saigon today. I just had enough time to have a

couple of drinks at a bar. Me and Ball meet a girl that works with the 450 at Cam Ranh, her name is Kathy and she's from New York. We had dinner with her, and then I met her at Saigon 450. We did a lot of walking today and I sure am tired. I went to the movies tonight.

**Day 276 February 11, 1969**
Well we were supposed to go back to Pleiku today, but there wasn't any flight going out of Bien Hoa airport today. We waited from 9:00 and until 4:30 PM. So we took a flight to Cam Ranh Bay. We got there about 6:00, but we were on the wrong side, so we had to catch an Air Force bus to the other side. Then we ate supper at the snack bar, then we went to where you process out to go home to stay for the night. We just got back from watching the Bible, which is a very good movie. I saw Sgt. Carter at Bien Hoa. We leave in the morning for Pleiku.

**Day 277 February 12, 1969**
We left Cam Ranh this morning and arrived at this god forsaken place. I took off all day. Four of my best buddies, Wilbert, John, Ed and Arthur got picked up last night and they have to face a Court Marshall. We had a meeting tonight, and these damn lifers laid down the

law tonight. So I have to play it cool for the next 87 days. As of today, I will never smoke pot in this division for the rest of the time over here. They finally fixed our showers today, where we got cold and hot water. So this place is going to be hell to live in for the rest of my time here.

### Day 278 February 13, 1969

I was supposed to go to Camp Schmitt, but the C.O. wouldn't let us go. So I had to go with Lt. Lewis and cut down some lines. I climbed poles all morning long. I had guard duty this afternoon, and I made the man again. It's been so long since I've pulled guard, it's great. I went over to the club tonight. But I couldn't drink, so I guess I will never be a drunk, which is just fine with me. I wanted a jay so bad tonight I could taste it, but I am trying to stop, and I just hope I can. I am off all day tomorrow. My buddies got out of their Court Martial, maybe Jones has to face one.

### Day 279 February 14, 1969

I was off today because I made the man yesterday. This morning, I washed some clothes and I let Olson borrow them. This afternoon I had a pair of shades made for $9.90, then I went swimming which was just beautiful. Well I lied again, because tonight, I went out with Luncan, Knittle, Conklin, Link, and Jones and got super wrecked. I keep telling myself I've going to quiet, but seems it doesn't do any good.

## Day 280 February 15, 1969

Today or rather tonight was one of the happiest days of my life. Tonight my brother Jim called me from the 4th replacement, so me and Wilbert went down to get him. We went to some E-M club and had a soda, he had a beer. Then I brought him to my company. Then we went to the line shack where they were having a party. Jim had a couple of drinks, I introduced him to everybody over there, then we left. On the way back, Me, Jim, Wilbert, and John had a couple of jays, it was great to see my brother. Today I humped my ass off filling sandbags and some other odd shit. I have to go to Long Binh tomorrow to pick up Baxter and Tillerson.

**Day 281 February 16, 1969**

Me and Sgt. Bolsen had to leave this morning for Long Binh to pick up Baxter and Tilterson from L.B. jail, that place is for the birds. It took them about 30 minutes to clear and we got a ride back to Saigon, where we ate and then went to a civilian airport and had a coke. Those guys were really glad to get out of that place. They didn't really believe we were taking them out of there. We got a flight out of Saigon about 9:30 and went to Cam Ranh Bay. We have to stay in the airport all night because there isn't any way we can get to the 22nd replacement. We had to ride through Saigon with a 45 in my hand.

**Day 282 February 17, 1969**

We had to sleep on some chairs last night and boy was I sore today. Our flight left about 9:00 this morning, and stopped at Nha Trang, then we arrived at Pleiku about 10:45. I got back to the company about 12:00, ate chow and then took a shower. I was supposed to sign some kind of papers for my brother Jim to go home, but the C.O. was gone all day long. Brown took me to 4th med to get an ambulance to 71st FVAC. When I got here I ate a very good supper, but I could only eat about half of it. Then I wrote some letters and watched TV. I had to take four little yellow pills tonight. I wrote J.B. a nasty letter.

**Day 283 February 18, 1969**

I got a letter the day before yesterday from Wilbert's girlfriend Stean, wanting to know why Will wasn't writing. I got up this morning at 6:15 and had my x-rays taken at 8:00, but they didn't tell me what they read. I came back to the company and was off all day long. The doctor made my stomach hurt by sticking that tube up me rectum. I went over and got Jim and brought him over to the company I got those papers from the C.O. today and gave them to Jim, he gets out of this country anyway. I have to go back to the hospital on the 24th.

**Day 284 February 19, 1969**

This morning I went up to S-4 and got some new fatigues. I didn't work any this morning, I just stood around and ironed my clothes for guard duty this afternoon. Well, I made the man again today. So I went over and got Jim at about 7:30. Me, Jim, Jones, Knittle, Robinson, Link, and Luncan went out and got wrecked. Jim didn't leave until 10 till 11:00 tonight, so I sure hope he finds his way back before 11:00, for if he doesn't the M.P.'s will pick him up, but I don't think they'll do anything to him, at least I hope not. I sure hope he doesn't get into any trouble.

**Day 285 February 20, 1969**
I was off all day, I got up about 11:30 and went and ate chow. This afternoon me and Wilbert played some basketball and I passed the football. I went over to the 3rd & 12th to get Jim, but he had guard tonight. Me, Jones, Knittle, and Link went and got wrecked in the big culvert.

**Day 286 February 21, 1969**
Last night Charlie hit us, but his rounds were short. Today I had K.P. I didn't do any walk today except go on the raction run, and wash the NCO side. Jim came over tonight and while drinking at the E-M club he told me about Jeannie being in a car with two guys, and the amazing thing about it, it didn't even bother me. On the way to Jim house, Me, him and Mullins blew a couple of jays. Today I played a game of tackle, my team won 10–6.

**Day 287 February 22, 1969**

Well today, I did some work. First, I went over to where Jim is and we went and saw his 1st. Sgt. They are supposed to send his orders up to division. This morning and this afternoon I helped stack sandbags, then I helped put up a frame for a water tank behind the mess hall. Jim came over tonight, we just sat around and did nothing. Me & Mullins took him home about 9:30. I got a tape from my dad today, and I sent him one tonight. We're supposed to get to sleep in, in the morning.

**Day 288 February 23, 1969**

Well today was a good day, we got to sleep this morning, then I went to church. After church, Me, Link, Jones, and Grantham went to the hole and got wrecked. Then for some odd reason we got the rest of the day off. I just sat around and listened to some records. Jim came over tonight, so Me, him, Jones, Link, Grantham, and Mac went to the hole and got wrecked. Jim had to walk home, again which makes me feel very bad. All the villagers, and all the other Camps and Pleiku got hit last night, so that leaves us.

**Day 289 February 24, 1969**

Today was a very good day. I got up and made sure I made it to revelry, then went back to bed and got up at 10:30. I ironed some state side fatigues for it's all I have. The rest of the day I just sat around and waited for a ride to 4th med. I was surprised to get off today. Right now I am in ward 9 at 71st EVAC. At 8:20 some Lt. just came in and told these guys they're expecting Charlie to have a ground attack. So I might be fighting for my life tonight. I have to have many x-rays in the morning.

**Day 290 February 25, 1969**

This morning, I had to get up at 6:30 because Charlie was hitting the place. From there, I went to the x-ray room. I had to drink some pink shit, four glasses of it. I waited around most of the day to have my x-rays read. The doctor put his finger up my ass again today and it really hurt. He said I have some kind of infection. Came back to base camp and did nothing. Played some basketball with Ed and Auther. I traded my camera to Robinson for a recorder and $25.00 tonight. Taped some of my records. I am supposed to drive the C.O. tomorrow.

**Day 291 February 26, 1969**

Today was a very good day. I drove for the C.O. all I had to do was take him up to Battalion all day long. I received a letter from my buddy Jim Edmonds. Jim, my brother came over tonight, I drove him home in the C.O.'s jeep. Then Me, Link, and Jones rode around in the jeep and got wrecked on pot. From the looks of the village tonight it looks like it got hit hard. I just hope none of my buddies got hurt.

**Day 292 February 27, 1969**

I drove for the C.O. this morning. But his driver came back this afternoon. I sat in a tub of water because the doctor told me too. I got a good tan, I have to do this for 8 more days. I had to work at 6:00 tonight building these walls around our billets. Then me and Jim went to the show at the E.M club. Me, Link, and Jones walked Jim home and we all got wrecked on the way there. I finally received my card from my future wife, Jeannie.

**Day 293 February 28, 1969**

Today was payday, I drew $228.00. This morning I had to put sandbags in the walls and clean out the ditch. This afternoon, I sat in water, and tonight we had to change the billets around, now we all have a single bunk. I have fireguard tonight. We're all supposed to have an inspection in the morning. Jim came over tonight and got all drunk. Well, today I almost got shot. Johnson was cleaning his weapon and it was off safe and he had it pointed at my stomach with a round in the chamber. I am supposed to be billets orderly in the morning.

**Day 294 March 1, 1969**

Today wasn't a very bad day. This morning I got up at 20 till 3:00 with my stomach hurting. This morning I was the billets orderly. The Major just walked through the billets. This afternoon, I sat in some water on top of the bunker for about an hour. Then I went to sleep. I got my pictures back today. Tonight I took two more pills, which made me feel pretty good. We sat over at the E-M club and took them and drank some beers. We're supposed to go to the rifle range in the morning.

**Day 295 March 2, 1969**

Today was a pretty good day. This morning the guys went to the rifle range, but I didn't go. This morning I got my things ready for guard duty. I made the man again today, but it wasn't very easy, Calvin Stuart give me some competition. But the C.O. said I was dressed better than him, so I made it. I wrote Stean again tonight. Won a couple of dollars in poker tonight. I am off tomorrow morning.

**Day 296 March 3, 1969**

Today I was off all morning because I made the man yesterday. This morning, I slept until 11:45. This afternoon I went to the PX and bought me a pair of sunglasses and broke them tonight. I also got a pair of clear glasses fixed today. This afternoon, Me, Link, and Jones went out in a 2 1/2 (deuce and a half) and got wrecked. Tonight, Me, Link, Jones, Moose, and Muller went out and got wrecked. Today, I have 69 days left. Had to work during workcall.

**Day 297 March 4, 1969**

This morning I went on sick call to the 71st EVAC hospital. While I was down there they brought some Americans GI's in, and they were in bad shape. They also had two NVA. The doctor told me I have an ulcer, he gave me some medicine to take for it, and to come back in two weeks. He gave me a profile, which is good until I get my stomach fixed. Sgt. Mohn is making me the billets orderly. I got a letter from my old buddy.

Harvey Malloy today. It's been four days since I saw Jim, Me, Link, Jones, went out and got wrecked with Moose on the bunker line tonight.

**Day 298 March 5, 1969**

Today I was billets orderly, that's all I have to do now. I swept the place and ironed my fatigues for guard on the 7th, which I don't have to pull, but if I don't make the man I want pull any more, because of my profile. This afternoon I laid in the sun on top of the bunker. Then me and Dean went to the PX, and blew a jay on the way back. What's good about me having an ulcer is I don't have to do shit. Me, Jones, Moose, Mullen, McDowell and some other guy went out and got wrecked tonight, and boy Mac was really gone, we all were. I got my income tax papers from mom today.

**Day 299 March 6, 1969**

Today wasn't a bad day. I was billets orderly, again this morning. I just sat around and shined my boots. This afternoon I went to pick up my glasses. Then I went to Anne's and saw Jim there, he was wrecked. I got a manicure and shave while I was there. This afternoon Lt. Lewis told me I had to make the formations. Jim came over tonight, and then Me, Link, and Jones walked him home and stayed over there and bull shited for a while. My ulcer gave me a lot of pain tonight. I mailed my income tax today.

**Day 300 March 7, 1969**

Well this morning I was billets orderly again. I had guard this afternoon, but I made the man again. The C.O. at inspection, told me I was outstanding. I was the first one he picked for the man. Jim was over all afternoon. Me, Him, Link, and Jones went out and got wrecked on pot. We were so wrecked we couldn't find our way out of the place where we were smoking.

**Day 301 March 8, 1969**

I was so wrecked last night I fell asleep on my bunk with my clothes on. Today, I went to Camp Schmitt and Engineer Hill. Bought a couple of suitcases and a small tape recorder. I was off this morning anyway for making the man yesterday. This Evening, Jim came over, and Me, him, Jones, and Link went out and got wrecked again. I have never been as wrecked as I have last night and tonight. I couldn't go take a shower. I was so wrecked.

## Day 302 March 9, 1969

This morning when I got up I was still wrecked. I was so wrecked last night I felt like I was floating. I smoked about 13 jay with opium in them. We got to sleep in this morning. Sgt. Ivey and one new little punk Sargent gave us a bunch of lip, Me, Jim, Link, Jones and Luncan had a couple of jays before we went to church. Me, Jim, Shelhouse, Muller, Jones, Link, and some other guy from B Company went out and got wrecked, then we came back and got Mac and went out again.

## Day 303, March 10, 1969

I was billets orderly again today. I just sat around and did nothing. Cleaned my recorder and taped up all my recordings. This afternoon, Luncan and me went out in our bunker right next to our billets and blew a jay. If we had gotten caught we would be going to jail tonight. Me, Jones, Link, Jim, Grantham, Moose, and Anderson went out and got wrecked. I got a tape from Jeannie today.

## Day 304 March 11, 1969

This morning the C.O. caught me sleeping and asked me over to his office. He asks me all kinds of shit which makes me sick to hear. Then Sgt. Ivey that black son-of-a-bitch keeps bothering me. I have to watch the

Montagnards kids this morning. This afternoon, I am going to see my doctor. My doctor gave me some pills for my nerves. When I got back I found out I had guard duty today and that I missed guards mount. So I couldn't have made the man I have guard on the line, bunker 112.

**Day 305, March 12, 1969**

I had my last shift last night from 3–7, the only bad thing about having guard, it was chilly. I was off this morning, so all I did was sleep after I wrote Stean. This afternoon the C.O. told me he wanted me to be in charge of the day room. When they get it finished. This afternoon and this evening I had to paint our pisser. Tonight Me, Jim, Jones, Luncan, and Conklin went out and got wrecked on pot at our new hiding place. Last night was the first time I've had guard duty in a long time, I had it with two soul brothers.

**Day 306 March 13, 1969**

Today I had to help Sgt Mohn and Beavers in the day room. Lt. Lewis didn't want me to work too hard, so he let me paint our pisser between our billets and wire billets. I also painted during work call. Me, Jim, Luncan, Conklin, Jones, and Link went to the white room and got wrecked. Then we walked Jim home. For the past week or so I've been so wrecked I haven't been keeping my diary up, like right now it's Saturday the 15th I have fire guard tonight.

### Day 307 March 14, 1969

This morning I finished painting our pisser. Then I just stood around in the day room and watched the sergeants work. So I really didn't do any work today. Tonight Me, Jim, Jones, Link went out and got wrecked on pot. Then after we got back, Me, Link, Jones, Luncan, and Johnson went back to the white room and got more wrecked. I didn't have to pull fire guard last night for Sgt. Jeannings was on C.Q.

### Day 308 March 15, 1969

Well last night about 12:30 AM our white room burnt down. It was made out of all the rolls of cable we have. The only bad thing about it was we were the ones that burned it down. We left incense burning when we left. Today I had to paint our water heater. Then this afternoon I helped Sgt Beavers in the day room. Me, Jim, Link, Jones, McDowell, Moose, Muller, and Greenstien went to the hole tonight and got double wrecked. Me & Link were the only ones to walk Jim home tonight the rest were too wrecked.

**Day 309 March 16, 1969**

We got to sleep this morning and then I went to church, on the way I had a jay. I had guard today, but I made the man. Jim told me some more bullshit on Brownfield, so as far as I am concerned we don't know each other anymore and I just quit writing to her tonight. Me, Jim, Mac, Jones, Link, Mullens, Muller, Moose and Greensteen went out and got wrecked tonight.

**Day 310 March 17, 1969**

I was off this morning, because I made the man again yesterday. This afternoon, Charlie shot some sniper fire into base camp and shot a guy, so they made everybody stay in their billets. Lt. Lewis gave us a shake down this afternoon and now he wants us all to have clean and neat lockers. This is the first time in a long time that I haven't had any pot of my own. I've decided not to write to Jeannie any more until I get an answer from her concerning my letter I wrote last night about what my brother Jim told me.

**Day 311 March 18, 1969**

This morning I had to pull ESC on an A-24 a ¾ ton truck. Then Me, Jim, Jones, Luncan went up on the hill behind our billets and blew a ¾ pack of jays and boy were we wrecked when we came off it. This afternoon I went to pick up my profile, but they weren't open. This afternoon I just messed around in the day room. Lt. Lewis ran Jim out of our company today, because he's over here so much. Tonight Me, Jim, Jones, Conklin, Mac, Moore, and Muller went to the revenue and we almost got caught by the M.P. 's. Then we stayed over Jim's for a while and blew a couple of jays, then we almost got caught again on the way back.

**Day 312 March 19, 1969**

This morning I was the billets orderly because the general of the division was supposed to come around, but he didn't show up. This afternoon I went to get my profile, but I can't get it until tomorrow. This afternoon when I got back I didn't do anything. Lt. Lewis ran Jim off again today, he was only allowed to visit me during off duty hours. Right now I'm on C.Q. and I just finished typing Jeannie a letter. I'll be off all day tomorrow. This is the first time I've had C.Q. in a long time. I can't even remember when I had it last, I think it was in July.

**Day 313 March 20, 1969**

C.Q. wasn't bad last night because Link and Luncan came over and got me wrecked on pot. The 1st Sgt.

relieved this new Sgt. We have in our Houch, then an acting Sgt. came on. I went to bed this morning and got up about 1:30 and took a shower. They stopped the man today so now there isn't any way I can get out of guard duty. Tonight, ME, Jim and Jones went up on the hill and got wrecked. Then me and Arther went to the bunker line and saw Link on guard duty, then came and went to bed.

**Day 314 March 21, 1969**

This morning Charlie got us out of bed with a mortar and rocket attack. He hit about 150 yards from our company area, this is the first time he has come this close to us. This morning Jim came over and told me he was going to Hawaii for his next duty station (which is great news he's getting out of Vietnam). This morning I was billets orderly again. This afternoon, I went to 4th Med and picked up my profile. This afternoon, I cleaned up all the tables in the day room. Tonight Me, Jones, Jim, Link, Muller, Moose, Mullet and some other guy went out and got wrecked on pot. Then Me, Link, and Jones walked Jim home, Charlie is supposed to hit us again tonight.

**Day 315, March 22, 1969**

This morning Sgt Ivey made me billets orderly again. All I did was sweep the floor then I cleaned all my records. This afternoon I went to sleep at 11:30 and got up at 1:00 and then took a shower and got ready for guard. I have guard on the bunker line because that's where I wanted it. They don't have the man anymore, I have it in bunker 112.

**Day 316 March 23, 1969**

Yesterday I met one of the guys I went through AIT with, his name was Dorherty. I had guard for about five hours last night which wasn't too bad, just a little cold. I had it with McDowell and Olsen. Sgt. Ivey let us off today and I took a shower and went to bed. I got up at 12:00 and went and tried to eat but I couldn't eat. I am losing weight because I can't eat this army food. This afternoon me and Wilbert played some basketball. Tonight Me, Jim, Link, Jones and Conklin went out and got wrecked. All of us guys and Muller and Moose rolled the jays here in the barracks.

**Day 317 March 24, 1969**

Last night I had a bad trip on pot. I tried the scene of someone squeezing my chest to make me bold my breath and they did it too long and I passed out and when I did I fell and hit the ground and bounced. I messed up my shoulder and scratched my chin, plus hurt my jaw. This morning, I was billets orderly. This afternoon I went to the PX, and bought a recorder. Tonight they started the 6:00 formation again. I helped put two ice boxes in the day room. Well tonight Me, Jim, Link, Conklin, and Sgt Trabor were going across the field smoking a jay. The M.P.'s. came up. We all threw our jays away, but Conklin tried to hide the pack but the M.P. saw him and busted him, but they didn't take our names, they just took our stuff, they'll probably smoke, and keep the rest for themselves. We bought a $15.00 bag tonight.

### Day 318 March 25, 1969

After the cops left last night we went back and found our jays we threw away and smoked them. That was Charlie's first time to go out with us, and we all got busted by the cops. Tonight and this evening was one of the worse fucking days in my life. First, I got this stupid damn letter from Jeannie breaking us up, and then my damn brother hassles me so goddamn much, I couldn't even go out with him tonight and get wrecked on pot. He's supposed to leave tomorrow, today I was the billets orderly again, and this afternoon I went and helped paint the day room.

**Day 319 March 26, 1969**

This morning, I was the billets orderly again. This afternoon, I was the billets orderly again, because the General was supposed to come by, but he didn't make it. I helped paint in the day room this afternoon. Tonight, I went and saw a movie, it was titled Wild in the Streets. Then I went to the hill and got wrecked with Jones, Taylor, and Mullins. Jim came over today to say goodbye because he's going to Hawaii. I hated to see him go in a way, but it's better for him than to be here in the Nam.

**Day 320 March 27, 1969**

Today I worked all day in the day room getting it ready to open tonight. I was on guard today, but the C.O. is making me E-O. so I sold it to Luncan for $20.00. I worked in the day room tonight and it was a pretty good night. I came out right on my sodas and beer. Then after I closed the day room I went out with Mullins, Conklin, and some other guy, I didn't even know then we found Jones, Taylor and Link, but they had lost their bag. Comes to find out the new guy was supposed to be a C.I.D. (pig).

**Day 321 March 28, 1969**

For some odd reason they didn't get me up for revelry this morning, so I slept until 20 till 7:00. I cleaned up the day room this morning. They bought me 20 cases of sodas and 15 cases of beer today. I got two beautiful tapes from Jeannie tonight. They were the things I was waiting for, I taped her back but they didn't tape so I'll have to tape her again tomorrow. I brought in $29.10 tonight, a $1.40 over. So I should have it pretty easy for the remainder of my time over here.

**Day 322 March 29, 1969**

This morning I had to get up for revelry because it was mandatory. We got a new C.O. today. His name is Captain Doyal. I worked my ass off this morning cleaning up the day room, then I made Jeannie two tapes. I closed the day room at 3:00 today. Because the Red Cross girls are here. I brought in $28.50 tonight. I've got to say I have really got it made with this job. I got a letter from Stean today. This makes two days in a row I haven't had anything to smoke.

**Day 323 March 30, 1969**

I got up this morning at 8:30 because it was Sunday. I cleaned up the day room, and then I moved all my things up to Head Quarter billets just to get out of Ivey and Gaff's face because they both make me sick. It rained all day really hard. It filled my day room with water. I had to go pick up 20 cases of soda in the rain and I got soaked. I didn't open the day room until 7:00 tonight because I had too much work to do in it. After I closed tonight I went out with Muller, Mullett, Greenstien and a couple of other guys and got wrecked on pot, for the first time in three days.

**Day 324 March 31, 1969**

Today I cleaned up the day room and locked it up and didn't open it up until 6:30 because we were paid in it today. I packed up some things to send home today. I only drew $126.00 today, the clowns at finance screwed up my voucher. I wasn't very busy tonight. Me, Link were going to go out tonight, but the C.O. was still here so we didn't.

**Day 325 April 1, 1969**

Today I got up and cleaned the day room. Then Me, McDowell, Trabune, and Marcum went out and picked up the patrol. When I got back, Link, Jones, and Luncan got wrecked in the burn pit. I had to sell soda behind the bar while I was wrecked. After lunch,

Me, Jones and Mac went and smoked some more jays. Work was all right tonight, but time sure went by slowly. Right before I closed the day room, Me, Mac and Jones smoked a couple of jays on my patio. Boy, I was high all day long.

**Day 326 April 2, 1969**

Well this morning I cleaned up our billets, then I cleaned up the day room. Then Me, Link, Jones and Muller went to the PX, and on the way blew a couple of jays. I bought myself another tape recorder and a couple of albums. All I did the rest of the day was tape some sounds. After I closed tonight I taped some more. Robinson tried to get me to go out tonight, but I didn't want to go, so I didn't. I'll have to pick up some sodas and beer tomorrow.

**Day 327 April 3, 1969**

This morning I cleaned up my day room and then taped some more sounds for my recorder. Me, Link, and Luncan went up on the hill behind 5/16 and got wrecked on pot before lunch. After lunch I just sat around in the day room and listened to my tapes right before I opened back up at 5:30. I had a couple of more jays. After I closed, me and Conklin went and found

Jones, Luncan, Taylor and Link. We stayed there until 12:00 and got really wrecked. That was the first time I have ever been AWOL, but they didn't catch me.

**Day 328 April 4, 1969**

This morning nobody got me up for revelry so I slept through it. This was the first time I had ever done this. I taped some more records, and then had to go pick up 20 cases of soda, and 15 cases of beer. On the way, me and Luncan had a couple of jays. I worked in the day room the rest of the day. I didn't open the day room until 7:00 tonight, that's when it opens where the C.O. works. I sold a lot of beer and soda tonight. After I got off work I went looking for the guys but I couldn't find them so I had a jay by myself.

**Day 329 April 5, 1969**

Today I cleaned up the day room after I got up at 7:30 because they didn't get me up for revelry again. I taped some more records this morning. I closed the day room at 3:00 today because the Donut Dollies were here. Then Me, Link, Jones, went behind the E-M club and had a few jays. After I closed the day room tonight, Me, Luncan, Robinson, and Taylor went up on the hill behind 5/16 and got wrecked on pot.

**Day 330 April 6, 1969**

We got to sleep in this morning until 8:30. Today was Easter, and I didn't even go to church. There were all kinds of people in the day room this morning so I just left it open. After I closed tonight Me, Jones, Link, Luncan, Robinsons and Taylor went up on the hill and got wrecked on pot.

**Day 331 April 7, 1969**

This morning I missed revelry again, but I got away with it. I got up at 8:00 and went and cleaned up the day room. Then I went to finance and they are going to pay me next month the money they shorted me this month. I went out with Link after dinner and got wrecked. After I got off work tonight I went out with Luncan, Taylor and Mims and got wrecked on pot.

**Day 332 April 8, 1969**

Well I had to get up this morning to piss in the bottle, to make sure I've been taking my pills they make us take while we're over here, then I went back to bed and got up about 9:00 and cleaned up the day room. Then Me, Muller, Greenstine had an appetizer before lunch (that's a jay). They gave me some new times for opening the day room 12:30 to 5:00 and 6:00 to 10:30. But

I close at 10:00. While I was working tonight, Muller and I went out and had a jay. I didn't go out tonight, because I couldn't find any of the guys.

### Day 333 April 9, 1969

This morning, I missed revelry again and got away with it. I cleaned up the day room. I was supposed to get some soda today, but they were closed. I played pool all day long. Tonight while I was working in the day room, Tommy Taylor bet me $100.00 that I wouldn't smoke a jay behind the bar in the day room, so I did with all of these people in there. So I won $100.00 on the bet. I didn't go out tonight. I just sat around at cable section and ate a lot of food.

### Day 334 April 10, 1969

This morning Sgt Walker made me get up and watch the Montagnards kids until lunch. After lunch I played pool and ping pong all afternoon. Tonight while I was selling beer, Leach, a soul brother, came in and gave me a jay. After work, Me, Jones, Robinson, Luncan, Daurtry and his buddy Greenstien, Davis, Laufooch, Moose, and Mimms all went out and smoked some jays, bowls, and toothpicks, we were all wrecked when we came off of the hill. I decided not to extend my stay over here today. During work tonight Sgt. Trabue came in wrecked, and I was nice, so we had a ping pong ball fight.

## Day 335 April 11, 1969

Well I made it for revelry again this morning, but afterwards I went back to bed until 10:00. When I got up I went and emptied a trash can, then I received 20 cases of soda and 10 cases of beer. I didn't smoke any tonight while I worked. I received a letter from my brother Jim today. After I closed tonight I went out with Link, Luncan, and Daurtry and we had three jays apiece. Me and Mims kept the guys awake tonight making noise in the billets.

## Day 336 April 12, 1969

Well today I got up for revelry, but I went back to bed until 10:00. Then I went and got a haircut. This afternoon, I closed at 3:00 and went to the PX. with Wilbert. I closed tonight and went out with Baxter, Mims, and their buddy from C-company, Jones and Greenstein, and smoked a bowl made out of a rock and really got wrecked on it.

**Day 337 April 13, 1969**

This morning we got to sleep in because it was Sunday. I slept until 9:30, and then I had to go and get some soda for the day room. Tonight, during work I slipped my index finger into my fan and it bruised up my finger, and cut it a little, then me and Mims and Duncan went out and got wrecked on pot.

**Day 338 April 14, 1969**

This morning, I missed revelry and Lt. Grubbs warned me and two other guys. This morning, me and Mims mailed my recorder and another package home. Before lunch, me, Mims and Haymond went and smoked a pack of jays, I was wrecked. Tonight during work, I smoked a jay and after work me and Jones went down to the bunker line to see McDowell, Robinson, and Warren who were on guard duty, and got wrecked while we were down there. I finally got a letter from Jeannie today.

**Day 339 April 15, 1969**

Today I had to get up for revelry and piss in the bottle, but I didn't piss in it. This morning about 8:00 Charlie hit us with a rocket attack. The first one hit our mess hall and destroyed half of it. Some of my buddies were in it, like McDowell, Luncan, Warren, Muller, and a couple of cooks, luckily, no one was killed or badly injured except shrapnel from the rocket and wood. Me and Conklin ran over as soon as we could to help the guys. Now I think the C.O. wants to give me and three more guys the Bronze Star. I helped pile up what was left of the mess hall this afternoon. I wasn't open tonight, because we didn't have any power. Me, Robinson, Mac, Jones, and some other guys went out and got wrecked.

### Day 340 April 16, 1969

This morning Mims helped me clean up the day room. Then he and I went to Annes and got a massage and then I got a new crystal on my watch. This afternoon, I closed the day room at 4:00 to go eat at the mess hall in company C because we don't have one. Smoked a jay during work, but it didn't do anything for me. I didn't go out tonight, because nobody had any stuff, so tonight was a bummer. Found out today, I was going to Ft. Sill, Oklahoma, when I leave here.

### Day 341 April 17, 1969

This morning, Sgt. Walker got me up when he came back. Then I went and got some sodas and beer with

John, then this afternoon, I worked in the day room. Tonight, I went behind the com-center and smoked some pot. Then Me, Luncan and Mims went and ate. I sold my tape recorder and record player and all my records to Grantham for $30.00 tonight.

**Day 342 April 18, 1969**

This morning Mims helped me clean the day room. Then he and I went over to Anne's and got a manicure. On the way Me, him and Jerry Haymond smoked about 5 bowls of pot. This afternoon, I worked in the day room. This evening I had a work call and I had to help police around the mess hall. After work tonight, I went out and got wrecked on pot with some of my buddies, Mims, Cox, Muller, Mullet, Greenstein, Ward, and a couple of more guys. I am supposed to receive a medal tomorrow from the General of the division.

**Day 343 April 19, 1969**

Today, I had to get up and clean the day room because the general wanted to look at it. Today was the best day of my life as far as the army is concerned. Our division commander Major General Pepke awarded me with the Army Commendation Medal with a V device for valor.

Then I received my orders for Fort Sill. They gave me a four day drop, I leave here on the 6th of May. I had to go and get some sodas and beer this afternoon, and me and Lennie got wrecked. Tonight, after work I went out with Muller, Moose, Greenstein, Ward, Mims, and Davis, and got wrecked again. I was very honored to receive that medal today.

```
                    DEPARTMENT OF THE ARMY
                  HEADQUARTERS 4TH INFANTRY DIVISION
                       APO San Francisco 96262

GENERAL ORDERS                                          12 June 1969
ORDERS      3011

            AWARD OF THE ARMY COMMENDATION MEDAL FOR HEROISM

    1.  TC 320.  The following AWARD is announced:

WELCH, KENNETH R  RA11657257                    SPECIALIST FOUR United States Army,
Co A, 124th Sig Bn, 4th Inf Div, APO 96262
 Awarded:  Army Commendation Medal with "V" Device
 Date action: 15 April 1969
 Theater:  Republic of Vietnam
 Reason:  For heroism in connection with military operations against an armed
          hostile force in the Republic of Vietnam.  Specialist Four Welch dis-
          tinguished himself while serving with Company A, 124th Signal Battalion,
          4th Infantry Division.  On 15 April 1969, the 4th Infantry Division
          Base Camp came under rocket attack.  Specialist Welch who was working
          in the company day room, heard a loud explosion, and upon investigation,
          saw that his company's mess hall had sustained a direct hit.  Running
          to the mess hall, he worked with other personnel on the scene in ex-
          tracting trapped personnel from the wreckage.  He continued to probe
          the wreckage despite the continuing rocket attack, and the danger of
          explosion from leaking gas.  Specialist Four Welch's courageous acts,
          initiative and exemplary devotion to duty are in keeping with the
          highest traditions of the military service and reflect great credit
          upon himself, his unit and the United States Army.
 Authority:  By direction of the Secretary of the Army, under provisions of
             AR 672-5-1.

        FOR THE COMMANDER:

                                    GORDON J. DUQUEMIN
OFFICIAL:                           Colonel, GS
                                    Chief of Staff

J. R. SIMEK
CPT, AGC
Asst AG

DISTRIBUTION:
 6 AVDDH-AGD
 2 AVDDH-ASD           1 CG, USARV, ATTN: AVHAG-DB, APO 96375
 2 Indiv conc          1 USA Mers Svc Support Center
 1 Indiv 201             ATTN: AGPE-F, Fort Benjamin
 5 124th Sig Bn          Harrison, Indiana 46249
```

## Day 344 April 20, 1969

We got to sleep in this morning until 8:30 and then Sgt. Walker came and got me up. I just sat around and bullshited all morning after I cleaned my day room. Today was pretty slow, nothing much happened. Tonight it rained. I didn't smoke any pot today. After work I went over to the com-center and listened to some sounds with my buddies. I didn't smoke any pot tonight either.

### Day 345 April 21, 1969

This morning, I cleaned up my day room and then I had to go get 20 cases of soda. I had to convert some money over, before I could buy them. Work wasn't too bad, I didn't have anything to smoke while I was working. After I got off work I went over to com-center billets and got wrecked on pot with Jones, Mullett, Muller, Ward, Greenstein, and two guys from B. company.

### Day 346 April 22, 1969

Today I got up for revelry and was supposed to piss in the bottle, but they ran out of bottles. I went back to bed and didn't get back up until 10:00 even though Sgt. Walker came through about 4 times telling me to get up. I didn't clean up the day room today. While I was working tonight, Cox gave me a jay and I went up to the burn pit and smoked it and got pretty high. Then after work, I went over behind com-center billets and got wrecked with Jones, Mullett, Moose, Ward, Muller, Greenstein, and Mims. We stoned the M.P.'s with rocks tonight.

**Day 347 April 23, 1969**

Today, I did the same thing I did yesterday, I went back to bed and didn't get up until 10:15. I was supposed to go get some sodas and beer today, but I couldn't find a driver so I didn't get any. After lunch today Me, McDowell and Luncan went for a walk and smoked two toothpicks apiece and got high. During work tonight I smoked a jay with so much opium in it turned the jay black. I cleaned up the place while I was wrecked. After work I went out with some of the guys from the com-center. This marked two days in a row, I didn't receive a letter from Jeannie after we made our agreement.

**Day 348 April 24, 1969**

This morning, I slept until 9:30, then got up and was supposed to go get some sodas and beer but I couldn't get a truck. This afternoon I got Williams to take me over and get some tonight. After work I went over behind com-center billets and got wracked with Mims, Luncan, Mullins, Muller, Mullitt, Greenstein, Moose, and Hutchinson. While we were wrecked we had so many good trips. I don't think I've ever tripped so much as tonight.

**Day 349 April 25, 1969**

This morning I slept until 9:00 and then me and Mims went and threw all the boxes away and emptied the trash cans in the day room. After chow this afternoon, I went out with Muller, Mullett and Moose and had a couple of bowls of pot. I got pretty high. I played pool and cards while I worked tonight. After work me, Mims, Mullins, Muller, Ward, Greenstein, Mullett, and Moose got wrecked and had some far out trips. Then me and Mims went to company C mess hall and got some milk and ham sandwiches.

**Day 350 April 26, 1969**

This morning, I got up at 7:30 and cleaned up the day room real good. I even washed the trash cans out. This afternoon Link and Jones came in. So then, Jones, Link, Mims, and myself went out and smoked a pack of jays. This afternoon, Mims had a trial and they gave him a year in jail (for bullshit). Sgt. Holley tended bar for me tonight, I just sat around and played cards. After work I went over to the com-center and got stoned with Muller, Mullins, Greenstein, Ward, Taylor, Mims and Bruce was there too. Then we all went over to the mess hall and got some food.

**Day 351 April 27, 1969**

This morning we got to sleep in so I slept until 9:30 and then cleaned up my day room. This afternoon Cox took me over to get some sodas and beer but they were closed. We smoked a couple of jays together and got stoned. I didn't have to do any work tonight, for I didn't have any sodas or beer. After work I went over behind the com-center and got stoned on pot with the regular gang. I am writing today's and tomorrow's diary on the 29th of April because I've been stoned on pot since then.

**Day 352 April 28, 1969**

Today I got up for revelry and then went back to bed until 10:30. I went and got some sodas and beer today with Mullins and some new dude. We rode around for a while because they weren't open until 3:00. I didn't do much work tonight because it was raining and nobody came in. Me, Jones, and Link smoked two jays in the day room. After work I went out with the regular gang plus Link, he came back today. For the past week, I've been hitting the stuff pretty hard, plus I've been going to bed at 12:00, 12:30 and 1:00 at night.

### Day 353 April 29, 1969

I got up this morning and then went back to bed until 10:30. They took Mims to jail today and I hate it. He was a very good friend of mine. I didn't clean the day room up today, just emptied some trash cans. I went over behind the com-center after lunch and got stoned on pot, work wasn't too bad tonight. After work I went over behind the com-center and got stoned with the rest of the guys. Luncan came back today and I got wrecked with him before work.

### Day 354 April 30, 1969

Today I got up and cleaned the day room because I thought they were going to pay us in there, but they paid us all in the orderly room instead. Me, Link, and Luncan went up on the hill and got stoned on pot, and we had to leave because the bugs were eating us up. I drew $351.00 today, but I had to pay out $150.00 for bills. During work tonight Me, Link, Lennie, and Muller smoked three bowls and then after work, I went over to the com-center and smoked some more, while we were eating in Mullets hooch, Lt. Warley came in and ran us to bed.

**Day 355, May 1, 1969**

Today I got up for revelry and then went back to bed until 7:30. Got up and went to the PX and Annies. I got myself a new watch band today at the PX. This afternoon I went to get some sodas and beer, but I couldn't get any sodas. Tonight they made me do work call and I had to shovel some dirt. Tonight while I was working Cox gave me three jays and me and Lennie smoked them. The guys almost got busted tonight by Sgt Nelson, so we didn't go out tonight. Lt. Grubbs tried to give me a hard way to go tonight because I didn't clean the day room, but I put him down while I was stoned.

**Day 356, May 2, 1969**

This morning I had to get up and clean the day room because Lt. Grubbs was digging in my shit this morning. I found some pot this morning and rolled my jays out of it. I gave all of them away except two, and they got me stoned. Then I had to go and get some sodas, the line was long and I had to wait until 3:30 to get them. I had to work at work call, until 7:30 tonight. I opened the day room at 8:15 and didn't get too much business. After work me and some of the guys from the com-center went out and got stoned on pot. Me, McDowell, Link and Jones stayed up until 12:30 listening to sounds. McDowell was really stoned tonight, the worst I've ever seen him.

**Day 357 May 3, 1969**

This morning I got up and cleaned the day room, then laid out in the sun for a while. I gave my job away today. So, today was my last working day. Me, McDowell and Link and Rossmess took the patrol out to the village and dropped them off. On the way back me and Link shot seven clips of ammo at cans on the side of the road. McDowell is supposed to go on a four day convoy tomorrow, so I'll be gone when he gets back. He's my best buddy over here. I wrote my last letter to Jeannie tonight.

**Day 358 May 4, 1969**

Last night I was so stoned on pot, I couldn't even walk. It was the worst I've ever been. Well today I started cleaning. I cleared everything except 201 files, and I will clear them tomorrow. This afternoon I had three jays given to me by John and I smoked two of them and I was really stoned while I was clearing finance. They had a party for the short timers at the line shack tonight, so I went up and ate a steak. I didn't get too stoned tonight because we went out late. Lt. Grubbs was the OD and he could have written us up, because we were out of bed at 11:00. I've only got four more days in this hell hole, to write in this diary, "Great."

### Day 359 May 5, 1969

This morning I went and cleared 201 files, then I just messed around the rest of the morning. Me, Link, and Luncan went up on the hill and smoked a giant jay. This afternoon I laid out in the sun and tried to get a tan. I had a pack of jays John gave me, so Me, Davis, Moose, and Peacock smoked them, so I've been wrecked since about 11:00. Tonight I went out with all the guys from the com-center. We smoked on the laundry porch. One more day in this sickening company.

### Day 360 May 6, 1969

This morning I went and pulled up my orders from 201 file, so all I have to do now is pick my ticket at 4th replacement in the morning. I laid out in the sun again today with Davis. Tonight at about 5:00 Me, Link, Davis, McDowell, and Luncan went to the water hole and smoked pot for about three hours. Tonight, I said goodbye to all my buddies by smoking with them.

Tonight is the last night I smoked with my buddies. I really hate to leave all my buddies over here.

### Day 361 May 7, 1969

Well today was the day. It was hard to say goodbye to my friends because I'll really miss them when I get home. McDowell, Link, and Luncan (three of my best friends in the room) took me to the 4th replacement, where I got my ticket and went to the air base. I was out of the 4th Division by 7:45 AM this morning. We didn't have any trouble getting a flight out of Pleiku, and arrived at Cam-Ranh Bay about 12:00. Just messed around, was processed in at the 50th replacement center. They told us we might not leave until our regular demos, which is the 10th of may. I sure hope not.

### Day 362 May 8, 1969

Today we got up at 7:00, had to go on police call and clean the billets. This afternoon I cleared everything and got ready for my flight home. As of right now I am going to close this diary of Vietnam with these words. It is 8:20 in the evening. I have just lifted off the ground of Vietnam, this was the LAST DAY. I am leaving this place called hell and heading toward heaven which is home to the ones I love. It was a good and experienced year, Specialist four Kenneth Rodney Welch.

P.S. This isn't in my diary, but my best kept secret from Vietnam is, me and my fiance Jeannie coordinated with each other with a three inch reel to reel tape recorder. When I would send her a tape, I would put some opium soaked joints in the tape container and when I got home I had a hundred joints to get me and my friend back home high.

When I got home and got off the plane at Greater Cincinnati airport I was picked up by my stepfather, mother and Jeannie. The first thing I noticed was that my mother had aged ten years. The worst part about coming home was, Coming Home.

The only thing I regret from the war, was I turned down the Bronze Star medal for the Army Commendation Medal. My agent Orange showed up on Jan 27, 2011, had triple bypass and four stents. I have ischemic heart disease.

To some, this memoir may not seem like much, but for a 19-year-old young man, it truly was an experience that will be with me always. Thank you

www.ingramcontent.com/pod-product-compliance
Ingram Content Group UK Ltd.
Pitfield, Milton Keynes, MK11 3LW, UK
UKHW022321100125
453395UK00002B/17